Now Playing:
Studying Western Civilization Through Film

Jonathan Perry
University of South Florida

New York Oxford
Oxford University Press

To Robert D. Craig
and to our shared love of film and history

Oxford University Press is a department of the University of Oxford. It furthers the University's objective of excellence in research, scholarship, and education by publishing worldwide.

Oxford   New York
Auckland   Cape Town   Dar es Salaam   Hong Kong   Karachi
Kuala Lumpur   Madrid   Melbourne   Mexico City   Nairobi
New Delhi   Shanghai   Taipei   Toronto

With offices in
Argentina   Austria   Brazil   Chile   Czech Republic   France   Greece
Guatemala   Hungary   Italy   Japan   Poland   Portugal   Singapore
South Korea   Switzerland   Thailand   Turkey   Ukraine   Vietnam

For titles covered by Section 112 of the US Higher Education Opportunity Act, please visit www.oup.com/us/he for the latest information about pricing and alternate formats.

Published by Oxford University Press
198 Madison Avenue, New York, NY 10016
www.oup.com

Oxford is a registered trademark of Oxford University Press

ISBN: 978-0-19-996987-6

Printing number: 9 8 7 6 5 4 3 2 1

Printed in the United States of America
on acid-free paper

TABLE OF CONTENTS

INTRODUCTION

Speaking about his experiences in writing the screenplay for *Danton* (1983), Jean-Claude Carrière observed that film is the only medium available for "recreating history." Because we cannot ourselves live in the past or see it for ourselves, he suggests, only the filmmaker can transport an audience back in time, at least to some extent. He concedes that *Danton*, like any other artistic product, also reflects its own time and that the context of Europe, and specifically of Poland, in the early 1980s must be taken into account in the film's interpretation today.

Furthermore, Carrière commented on the particular challenge he faced in reconstructing Danton's final speech to his accusers before being sentenced to death. As there is no surviving transcript of that speech, Carrière was obliged to craft a speech "that should have been said" on this occasion. Whether consciously or not, he was in this admission echoing precisely what Thucydides had claimed for his own speeches, set during the unfolding Peloponnesian War: "Some I heard myself, others I got from various places; it was in all cases difficult to carry them word for word in one's memory, so my habit has been to make the speakers say what was in my opinion demanded of them by the various occasions—of course, adhering as closely as possible to the general sense of what they really said." (Thucydides' *History of the Peloponnesian War*, I.22)

The main argument of this book is that an in-depth study of certain key films, set at formative moments in the history of Western Civilization, can help flesh out the details offered in a textbook treatment. The enormous power of film to shape perceptions of the past normally makes professors recoil in horror; it can be very annoying for a professor to explain, seemingly for the millionth time, that something a student has seen in a film and vaguely recalls for an examination is not "historically accurate." On the other hand, if handled with due caution, film can enhance the student's learning experience and lavish specific images, color, and sound upon elements that might seem lifeless on the textbook page.

The identification of the thirty films to be incorporated into this book, covering the entire span of Western civilization from its origins to the present, has been especially challenging. However, certain principles have guided the selection process. The first goal was to include directors from as many different national backgrounds as was feasible. While one could do a creditable job of analyzing only films made in the U.K., France, and the United States, the films described here have originated in those countries, but also in Denmark, Sweden, Poland, Canada, the USSR, Greece, Italy, and Spain.

A second factor involved the periods in which the films were produced. While the films addressed in this book include acknowledged classics of cinema by Dreyer, Bergman, and Kubrick, most were created in the past twenty-five years and several in the past five. This is partially because more recent films are more widely available, but it is also an acknowledgment that contemporary visions of the past continue—and will continue—to change with each generation of both directors and audiences.

Nevertheless, in spite of their geographic and chronological span, there are at least two themes that are consistently revisited in a number of them. A favorite topic among many directors throughout the twentieth and twenty-first centuries is the conflict between faith--usually described as hypersensitive, bullying, and violent--and reason, which appears to be calm, collected, but perhaps also naïve in the face of religious bigotry.

A second theme, and one that has emerged especially in response to the attacks of September 11, 2001 and the—very different—invasions of Afghanistan and Iraq that followed upon these attacks, involves the horrors of war. Filmmakers have often focused on those who suffer in war, and sympathy is sometimes elicited for one's enemies, by means of a long scream or a piece of music played for the victims of both sides of a conflict. Perhaps it is only when we realize that people on the "other" side of warfare also bleed when pricked that peace can be imagined.

Troy

Film Data

Year: 2004
Director: Wolfgang Petersen
Screenplay: David Benioff
Music: James Horner
Production Design: Nigel Phelps
Length: 162 minutes
Rating: R

Connection to *The Cultures of the West* by Clifford R. Backman

Chapter 4: "Greeks and Persians"

Preview

Troy bears very little resemblance to Homer's *Iliad*, and it is by no means a reliable introduction to the events chronicled in this Ur-text of Greek civilization. Nevertheless, the film is still worth viewing, particularly in respect to its mise-en-scène—as Western powers were again engaged in war in western Asia in the early twenty-first century—and to its director's fundamental vision of war's realities.

The *Iliad* opens with Achilles' wrath over the confiscation of his "prize," Briseis, by the Greeks' overlord Agamemnon, and it concludes with the abeyance of Achilles' wrath, when he bows to King Priam's plea to reclaim the body of his son Hector. The epic addresses only the final year—and not even the entirety of that year—in the ten-year-long struggle of the Greeks to reclaim Helen from the Trojans. This film, by contrast, attempts to cover the entirety of the war, from its origins to its conclusion by means of the Trojan Horse. Gratuitous errors mar the film as a whole, but it preserves some of Homer's original intentions. These may have been to demonstrate the need to sympathize with one's enemies, and to acknowledge that right and humanity may be on the other side as well as on one's own.

The film preserves some of the central episodes of the *Iliad*, developing the contrast between Achilles, who is weary with blustering commanders and the futility of war, and

Hector, who is equally noble and equally driven by his love for a woman. In this regard, the film is far less brave than Oliver Stone's *Alexander*, which was also released in 2004 and unapologetically underscored Alexander's bisexual behavior and perhaps his identity as well. In Petersen's *Troy*, Patroclus is merely Achilles' "cousin," and not his companion and lover. A safely heterosexual Achilles, in this context, may tell us more about contemporary attitudes toward sexuality than anything Homer's audience would have understood.

In interviews about the film, the German Petersen has referred to another German, the remarkable amateur archaeologist Heinrich Schliemann who, Homer in hand, had attempted to find the Troy of the *Iliad* in the late nineteenth century. Despite the sneers and dismissive attitudes of ancient historians, Schliemann—with the help of an underappreciated British enthusiast called Frank Calvert—found remnants of what could have been an actual Troy in modern northwestern Turkey. When he decided to film the Trojan War story, Petersen similarly turned to existing records, but also employed his imagination for a vaguely "Mycenaean" production design. Some elements in the royal palaces of Mycenae and Troy recall elements of actual Bronze Age archaeology, but others were imported from widely varying contexts, such as ancient Egypt, Mesopotamia, and Persia. Intrigued by the challenge of resurrecting the world of 1250 BCE, he combined these design elements into enormous sets, had hundreds of soldiers from the Bulgarian and Mexican armies trained in the "battle techniques" of the period, and employed new computer generated imaging technology to flesh out the details.

Having shot some of the film in Malta, Petersen hoped to shoot the remainder on Morocco's Atlantic coast. However, the turmoil that came to shake the Middle East, accelerated by the invasion of Iraq in early 2003, necessitated a change of venue. Petersen moved production to Mexico's Baja California and weathered a hurricane and other natural and manmade disasters. Thus, modern warfare actually shaped the making of this film, and the present may never have been far removed from Petersen's original conception. Petersen observed how difficult it was for his actors and the extras to bear up under brutal sunshine, heat, and constantly pouring sweat, observing, "Our battles are not glorious."

Perhaps the theme of this film is that, regardless of how long one's name lives on in history books and in epic poetry, war is never a glorious exercise. Petersen had first come to international attention for his searing portrait of German sailors trapped in a submarine during World War II in 1981's *Das Boot* (*The Boat*). By sharing the suffering of "the enemy," one can experience the indignities and the horrors of war, on all sides of a conflict. Thus, while the gods are conspicuously absent from Petersen's *Troy*, larger themes of war and its true nature abound in the piece.

Recommended Scenes

➢ Hector discovers that his brother Paris has lured Helen away from her husband Menelaus, and Menelaus offers his brother Agamemnon a perfect pretext for a war on Troy, 00:16:20 through 00:21:15.

➢ While the image was pared down from its original conception, a CGI shot of the flotilla of Greek ships and their initial landing on Troy's beaches is offered between 00:35:48 and 00:44:31.

➢ Achilles confronts the warmonger Agamemnon over his confiscation of Briseis, 00:53:42 through 00:56:34.

➢ Hector kills Patroclus, who is wearing Achilles' armor, and Hector prepares for the final conflict by comforting his wife Andromache and their infant Astyanax, 01:43:18 through 01:50:35.

➢ The highlight of the film is the final duel between Hector (played by Eric Bana) and Brad Pitt's Achilles, 01:57:37 through 02:03:30. The battle is effectively choreographed, and is completely the work of the actors themselves—with the accentuated sound of swords whizzing through the air.

➢ A regal Peter O'Toole, playing Priam, comes to Achilles' tent to beg for Hector's body, 02:05:20 through 02:11:55. Achilles grieves over the corpse of his great enemy, as well.

Discussion Questions

1. Does the film bear out its director's observation that there is nothing "glorious" about war?

2. What contemporary allusions may *Troy* have been making, to the world of 2004?

3. How does the film reinforce the concept of respect for one's enemies?

Further Reading and Viewing

Petersen's *Das Boot* (1981) introduces similarly ambiguous themes of war and its justification, as does his *In the Line of Fire* (1993), a reflection on presidential security told through the weary eyes of a U.S. Secret Service officer.

The best analyses of the film can be found in Martin M. Winkler's edited volume *Troy: From Homer's Iliad to Hollywood Epic* (Blackwell Publishers, 2007). Particularly remarkable in this book are the essays by J. Lesley Fitton, "*Troy* and the Role of the Historical Advisor," pp. 99–106 (which asks whether a historical advisor would have made any difference in the end result), and, in delightfully ironic mode, Jon Solomon's "Viewing *Troy*: Authenticity, Criticism, and Interpretation," pp. 85–98.

The Trojan Women

Film Data

Year: 1971
Director: Michael Cacoyannis
Based on Euripides' tragedy, translated by Edith Hamilton
Music: Mikis Theodorakis
Length: 106 minutes
Rating: No rating

Connection to *The Cultures of the West* by Clifford R. Backman

Chapter 5: "Hellenistic and Second Temple Judaism"

Preview

The renowned classical scholar Edith Hamilton opened her 1937 essay entitled "A Pacifist in Periclean Athens" with the claim that, "The greatest piece of anti-war literature there is in the world was written 2,350 years ago." Euripides' *The Trojan Women*, probably produced for the first time at Athens in spring 415 BCE, has generally been interpreted as a direct artistic response to Athens's brutal treatment of the inhabitants of the island of Melos the previous year. While some have argued that the connection is not so explicitly made, the parallels between the sufferings of the people of Melos—particularly its women and children—and the women and children of Troy after it has been sacked seem inescapable. *The Trojan Women* is one of the few plays by Euripides that have survived, and the other two tragedies in the original trilogy (three plays, plus a "satyr" play, were typically offered at the same time into competition in the fifth century) are lost.

　　Nevertheless, the play is often read in conjunction with Thucydides' penetrating and disturbing account of the Athenians' conquest of tiny Melos, which had tried to remain neutral amidst the titanic Peloponnesian War that had engulfed the Greek world. Thucydides' famous "Melian Dialogue" envisions the protests a small power might make against a more powerful one, and yet the section ends with the bald statement of fact: "The Athenians killed all the men of military age and enslaved the women and children. Then they

colonized the island, sending five hundred settlers of their own for the purpose."
(Thucydides 5.116)

Turning back to the origins of Hellenic civilization and its foundational legends, Euripides profiles the sufferings of all of Troy's women (symbolically offered in the "Chorus" of Trojan Women after whom the play is named), but particularly of Queen Hecuba, her daughter Cassandra, and her daughter-in-law Andromache. Helen is in a rather different category, but the play is composed of a series of laments, choral odes, and three scenes involving Cassandra, Andromache, and Helen. On the other side of the conflict stand the Greek men, including Helen's jilted husband Menelaus and, most strikingly, the "reasonable" Talthybius, who is a persistent bringer of increasingly unwelcome news.

The murder of the young boy Astyanax, the child of Hector and Andromache who is thrown from Troy's wall to prevent his growing up and seeking revenge, is the culminating act of the play, but it happens, as per Greek conventions, off-stage. Cassandra's commentary on the futility of war and the wrenching laments of Andromache and Hecuba, in particular, have echoed over the centuries, and *The Trojan Women* has repeatedly inspired new artistic interpretations, especially in the midst of contemporary conflicts. Jean-Paul Sartre adapted the story in 1965 as *Les Troyennes* and in his introduction deliberately compared the suffering inflicted by the French government and military on the people of Algeria in recent years. The finest version of the play now available is Michael Cacoyannis's visceral statement dedicated, as he notes at the film's conclusion, "to those who resist the oppression of man by man." In his own introduction to the screenplay, Cacoyannis noted that the "takeover by a military regime in Greece"—the "junta" of generals who, backed by the U.S. government, terrorized Greeks between 1967 and 1974—had inspired him to revisit Euripides. In his estimation, Euripides' *The Trojan Women* represented a shared "need, stronger now than it had ever been before, to cry out against oppression in any shape, place or form." In the wrenching scream of Vanessa Redgrave's Andromache, realizing that her child will be murdered by her enemies, many observers in 1971 and in much later times have heard the inexpressible pain of those who are shattered by war.

Recommended Scenes

➤ The film opens with a description of the scene of Troy's women and children fleeing from the smoking ruins of their city—accompanied by the breathtaking music of the contemporary Greek composer Mikis Theodorakis, 00:00:59 through 00:08:55. Hecuba, magnificently played by Katharine Hepburn, forces herself "Up, up from the ground."

➤ Hecuba interacts with the Chorus of women as they speculate about their disastrous futures, 00:10:50 through 00:12:51.

➤ Cassandra (Genevieve Bujold), whom everyone presumes is mad but is actually inspired by the god Apollo, performs her "marriage" rites, 00:23:25 through 00:35:02. She predicts—and the audience knows this to be the case—that she will be murdered in the home of her new Greek master, Agamemnon, but she comes out of her ravings to make a profound comparison of Trojan and Greek soldiers in this conflict.

➤ Andromache and Hecuba compare their respective griefs, 00:48:04 through 00:53:29.

➤ The pivotal scene of the film is the announcement to Andromache that her "child must die," 00:53:30 through 01:06:04. Vanessa Redgrave conveys the grief from deep inside her through a long and growing scream, but her little son is pitilessly led away to his death.

➤ The cause of the war, Helen, appears through the slats of a wooden cage and, with perfect hauteur, bathes herself while the women of Troy wail in agonies of thirst, 01:07:29 through 01:10:20.

➤ Variously penitent and seductive, Helen (Irene Papas) convinces her husband to spare her life, and, despite Hecuba's insistent appeals to kill her, she survives, 01:18:58 through 01:26:04.

➤ Hecuba grieves over the corpse of her grandson Astyanax, commenting on "this fear that comes when reason goes away," and the women are led away to their new lives of slavery and exile, 01:30:17 through 01:46:05.

Discussion Questions

1. Does the film directly comment on conflicts that were raging in the late 1960s and early 1970s?

2. What is the message of Cassandra's frenzied speech in the cave?

3. What does the film suggest about the putative "causes" of conflicts?

Further Reading and Viewing

A tie-in book, including Edith Hamilton's translation of *The Trojan Women*, Cacoyannis's screenplay, essays by Hamilton and Cacoyannis, and photographic stills from the film, was published by Bantam Books in 1971. For scholars' doubts about the precise connections between Euripides' play and the massacre of the Melians, see especially A. Maria Van Erp Tallman, "Euripides and Melos," *Mnemosyne* 40 (1987): 414–419.

Cleopatra (1963)

Film Data

Year: 1963
Director: Joseph L. Mankiewicz
Music: Alex North
Length: 246 minutes
Rating: No rating

Connection to *The Cultures of the West* by Clifford R. Backman

Chapter 5: "Hellenism and Second Temple Judaism"

Chapter 6: "The Empire of the Sea: Rome."

Preview

This spectacle that sunk Twentieth-Century Fox into a morass of financial loss and moral scandal is little appreciated today for its cleverness and originality. Centered on the tempestuous personal relationship between its stars, Elizabeth Taylor and Richard Burton, publicity for the film and Taylor's costumes, wigs, and makeup overwhelmed the historical scenarios it attempted to reproduce. Although Taylor and Burton were both married at the time, they fell, perhaps like Antony and Cleopatra, deeply and headlong into passion for each other. Delays set in, Taylor experienced several setbacks to her health, and the production became known as a bottomless money pit before it was finally released in 1963. Like Cecil B. DeMille's *Cleopatra* (1934), which it was clearly designed to answer, Mankiewicz's *Cleopatra* updated the language and contemporized the relationships, in the process revealing changing attitudes (and some progressive and enlightened ones) regarding women's roles in 1960s society.

It is easy to focus more on Taylor's dizzying array of costume changes than on the subtlety of her performance as an intelligent and competent ruler in her own right. Particularly in her scenes with Rex Harrison, playing a world-weary but bemused Julius Caesar, Taylor underscores the dignity of Cleopatra and her single-minded determination to preserve and extend Egypt's power. From the famous rug scene and throughout the first (and better) half of the film, her Cleopatra displays scientific curiosity, political acumen, and a comprehensive vision of a cosmopolitan world, which she associates with the legacy of Alexander the Great. Particularly determined to safeguard the interests of her son with Caesar, Caesarion—although her union with Antony is surprisingly, and ahistorically, childless in the film—this Cleopatra ultimately fails in her goals. Occasionally carried away in torrents of emotion for Antony, she generally seems a stronger, more determined character than her Roman partner, and he degenerates into a dependent force who cannot defend her from her enemies.

The film's title sequence stresses its fidelity to primary sources by claiming to be "based upon Hhistories by Plutarch, Suetonius, Appian, and other ancient sources," together with Carlo Maria Franzero's 1957 biography, *The Life and Times of Cleopatra*. This fidelity is not always apparent and the screenplay contains clunky dialogue at times, but the surviving film is a much truncated version of what Mankiewicz had originally intended. At least one further hour of material was shot for each half of the film (the relationship with Caesar was thus intended to parallel the relationship with Antony), and the development of the characters is rendered more impressionistic in the film's final cut. Nevertheless, the film nicely develops the contrast between Cleopatra (and Antony, to a lesser extent) and Octavian, brilliantly imagined by Roddy MacDowall. The tragedy of Antony and Cleopatra is borrowed from Shakespeare but refashioned to address the concerns of modern women in a world dominated by men.

Recommended Scenes

➤ The film opens on the battlefield of Pharsalus (mistakenly labeled "Pharsalia") in 48 BCE and parallels the civil war between Caesar and Pompey with that between Cleopatra and her brother Ptolemy. It contains a dazzling overhead shot of a recreated harbor at Alexandria and introduces Ptolemy and his advisors. Borrowing from Plutarch's *Life of Caesar,* chapter 48, Caesar is presented with the head of Pompey—although he doesn't visibly weep over his signet ring, as in Plutarch—between 00:15:08 and 00:18:02.

➤ The expected scene of a rug unraveled to reveal Cleopatra to Caesar is offered between 00:19:34 and 00:27:04. In this version, however, Cleopatra emerges from her rug and instantly begins speaking about Egypt's political situation. The stress is not, as in Plutarch's chapter 49, on her seductive charms, but rather on her no-nonsense approach to Egyptian and Roman interests.Cleopatra is conferring with her scientific advisor and personal tutor Sosigenes when she hears of the (accidental) burning of the library at

Alexandria by Caesar's troops, 00:38:57 through 00:43:54. Her outrage over the "barbaric" burning of "human thoughts" is palpable, despite Caesar's weary attempts to help the "young lady" understand his position.

➤ A particularly attractive scene—though much pared down from its original version—takes place between Caesar and Cleopatra before a beautifully imagined tomb of Alexander, 01:01:50 through 01:06:06. Cleopatra brings up the story of Caesar's weeping before a statue of Alexander in Spain, when he realized he had not achieved so much at his age, and the production designers have recreated the famous fresco of the Battle of Issus for the shrine's walls. Her certainty that she will bear Caesar a son is connected to her vision of a new blended Roman and Hellenic world.

➤ Cleopatra enters Rome in one of the film's centerpieces (despite the insertion of an ahistoric Arch of Constantine, not built for another 350 years), 01:21:22 through 01:31:04. In a clever interpretation of the assassination of Caesar, Cleopatra witnesses the scene through a sorcery-inspired vision, 01:48:31 through 01:55:21. Unlike DeMille's version, this film stresses that Cleopatra and Antony had known each other in Rome—and that Antony was instrumental in persuading her to leave Rome before the mob could attack her and Caesarion.

➤ [The following scenes are found on the second disc, with times beginning again.]

➤ Octavian and Antony are shown making plans in Octavian's tent at Philippi, and Cleopatra makes her own plans in Egypt, 00:04:18 through 00:06:20.

➤ The barge scene in Tarsus is less fantastic than DeMille's, but still worth viewing, between 00:10:05 and 00:12:34.

➤ Cleopatra makes demands on Antony, and the Donations of Alexandria are contrasted with the propaganda machine of Octavian in Rome, 00:52:30 through 01:02:38. In one of the film's most visceral scenes, Octavian whips up the mob and casts a spear launching war against Cleopatra. This is true to history, but the film adds a twist by having the spear cast into the body of Cleopatra's tutor Sosigenes.

➤ The Battle of Actium (31 BCE) is depicted—despite unrealistic models for Cleopatra to examine—in a creditable manner, 01:08:20 through 01:21:12. In contrast to Shakespeare's derisive "picking up her skirts and rushing away," this Cleopatra leaves the scene of battle and is ignominiously followed by Antony only because she hears that Antony is dead and is determined to protect her son from the Romans.

➤ The final scenes of Shakespeare's *Antony and Cleopatra* are depicted, with some language borrowed and reiterated from the play, between 02:04:40 and 02:08:53.

Discussion Questions

1. Does the film provide commentary on the changing roles of women in 1960s society? What motivates Cleopatra the most, at least in Taylor's portrayal of her?

2. What does the film suggest about the intersection of seduction and political power? Would a male monarch have been as effective as Cleopatra, in relation to Caesar and Antony?

3. What role does Octavian play in this story? Why?

Further Reading and Viewing

Mankiewicz's version of the film is analyzed and compared with DeMille's in Maria Wyke's *The Roman Mistress: Ancient and Modern Representations* (Oxford University Press, 2002), pp. 302–315. Wyke connects the scandal of Burton's and Taylor's betrayal of marriage vows with Roman attitudes to the Egyptian "mistress."

Warrior Queen

Film Data

Year: 2003
Director: Bill Anderson
Screenwriter: Andrew Davies
Length: 86 minutes
Rating: No rating

Connection to *The Cultures of the West* by Clifford R. Backman

Chapter 6: "The Empire of the Sea: Rome."

Preview

Roman Britain, in particular, has proven an especially fertile place in which to plant the Roman genre film and especially in the past decade. This film, like many still to be analyzed, sprang up in the shadow of 9/11 and in the preparation and rapid implementation of the invasion plan for Iraq by the "Coalition of the Willing" in early 2003. *Warrior Queen* is thus, ultimately, a film about the consequences of imperialism and how one nation's "terrorists" (a word used repeatedly in the script) can also be considered "defenders of their land." Although not a terribly sophisticated film and decidedly lacking in production values—and marred by bizarre music and religious ceremonies—the film marks a sharp turn in the applicability of Rome to modern times.

While other films—one thinks of *Ben-Hur* (1959) and *Monty Python's "Life of Brian"* (1979)—have examined, for both tragedy and comedy, the lives of conquered peoples in the Roman Empire as a whole, *Warrior Queen* draws attention to the nobility, and perhaps even the necessity, of resistance to Rome. This is especially fraught territory for the contemporary United Kingdom, as Prime Minister Blair had pledged his nation to support President Bush of the United States in the lead-up to invading Saddam Hussein's Iraq, against the wishes of a significant portion of his people. The U.K. might serve, ironically, as a symbol of both imperial power—as the former colonial overlord in Iraq—and as a resistor to the imperial power of Rome, since the image of "Britannia" was adapted, in part, from the image of the famous Boudicca (Boadicea in some versions).

This queen of the Iceni people took command after the death of her husband Prasutagus and, assisted by her two daughters, launched a revolt against Roman authority c. 61 CE during the reign of Nero. The image of Boudicca in her war chariot has been and remains instantly recognizable in today's Britain, as there is a remarkable statue of her and her daughters alongside the Thames, designed by the artist Thomas Thornycroft and installed in 1902. The statue appears at the conclusion of *Warrior Queen*, together with the suggestion that one of Boudicca's daughters has now been resurrected and walks by the statue in contemporary London, offering an enigmatic smile to the viewer.

The film affords some, though generally inadequate, consideration to the motives and goals of the Roman occupiers of Britain, but it focuses most attention on the personal life and grievances of Boudicca and her family. Virtually everything known about Boudicca is contained in Tacitus's *Annals* 14.31–35, and she appears, as do most of Tacitus's foreign opponents, as a noble enemy to a corrupt Principate. According to Tacitus—whose own father-in-law Agricola was later, it should be remembered, a governor of Britannia—the various peoples of Britain were reacting individually and restively to the invasion of their island by Roman forces under Claudius in 43 CE. Prasutagus, King of the Iceni, had named the Roman Emperor and his daughters joint heirs upon his death, in a move presumably designed to ensure his people's survival and to demonstrate his loyalty to Rome.

Nevertheless, Roman authorities committed an outrageous act of savage beating and rape against Boudicca and her daughters, triggering a wide-scale revolt that destroyed several Roman towns and nearly drove the Romans out of their newly-acquired province. After a final battle against Boudicca—the general consensus of archaeologists is that it took place near Mancetter in the English Midlands—the Romans re-established control. They were now, however, forced to acknowledge that subduing an occupied enemy would be far more difficult than simply invading and declaring victory.

Recommended Scenes

➢ The film begins with a voiceover prologue spoken by Boudicca, while her husband is still alive. She insists that the Romans came "to *our* land," and the next scene shows an attack on Roman forces (and specifically the historically-appropriate 14th Legion) by British children. In negotiation with Prasutagus, a Roman diplomat labels the move by the children "cowardly terrorism," which Prasutagus counters with, "We call it defending our home," 00:04:22 through 00:10:40.

➤ The will of Prasutagus is read to Boudicca, and the Roman authority continues to stress that hers is a "subject people" whose "acts of terrorism" can no longer be tolerated. When she continues to defy him, he orders Boudicca to be whipped while witnessing the rape of her daughters by a host of Roman soldiers. This is a horrifically graphic scene, both physically and emotionally, and should be screened with care, 00:35:47 through 00:43:25.

➤ In the first stage of her revolt against the Romans, Boudicca launches the destruction of the Roman town Camulodunum, and her calm, effective leadership is contrasted with that of the rash youth Nero in Rome, 01:01:29 through 01:04:25.

➤ In one of the few glimpses the film offers of the Romans' side of the conflict—beyond the erratic megalomania of Nero—the governor Suetonius asks, "Why are we here?" Some of the Romans seem to find the Britons' resistance heroic, if futile, and thus begin to doubt the wisdom of their own occupation effort, 01:09:30 through 01:10:42.

➤ Contrasting speeches by Boudicca and the Roman Suetonius are offered before the final battle. One might think this was inspired by *Braveheart* or *Gladiator*, but the notion of dueling speeches is actually derived from Tacitus, *Annals* 14.35–36. Suetonius acknowledges that Boudicca is "a worthy opponent," but she and at least one of her daughters are lost in the battle, 01:14:01 through 01:25:10.

Discussion Questions

1. Does the film suggest that Boudicca's motives in seeking revenge against the Romans were personal? Would she and her people have been better off acquiescing to Rome's demands?

2. Do the Romans have long-term goals in Britain, or are they simply afraid to look weak in the eyes of others if they withdraw?

3. Are the comments on "terrorism" appropriate for a film, regardless of its period and place, in the aftermath of 9/11?

Further Reading and Viewing

There has been a spate of books about Boudicca in the past decade, many inspired directly by this film and its attendant publicity. The best among them is probably Richard Hingley and Christina Unwin, *Boudica: Iron Age Warrior Queen* (Hambledon Continuum, 2006).

Quo Vadis

Film Data

Year: 1951
Director: Mervyn LeRoy
Based on the novel *Quo Vadis?* (1896), by Henryk Sienkiewicz
Music: Miklos Rozsa
Historical Advisor: Hugh Gray
Length: 174 minutes
Rating: No rating

Connection to *The Cultures of the West* by Clifford R. Backman

Chapter 7: "Paganisms and Christianities."

Preview

According to Roman Catholic legend, Peter the Apostle was departing from Rome in the summer of 64 CE when he was confronted by a man resembling the Jesus whom he had known three decades earlier. When he asked, in Latin, *"Quo vadis, Domine?,"* "Whither goest thou, Lord?," Jesus responded that he was returning to Rome to be crucified a second time and then disappeared. Peter acknowledged the divine lesson and returned to comfort the Christians of Rome, who were scapegoated by Nero in the wake of the Great Fire of Rome. The story was critical for Catholic claims of Peter's sovereignty over the church, as he was believed to have been crucified on Vatican hill during this persecution. Nevertheless, the wider story of Christian persecution by Nero in 64 is not merely a church legend; the main source for it is the non-Christian (and even vehemently anti-Christian) historian Tacitus, who highlights the suffering of this sect in his *Annals* 15.44.

The narrative of the Great Fire of Rome and the concomitant persecution—on a localized but graphically violent scale—of Christians was a sufficiently dramatic story for a host of novels, stage plays, and, eventually, films. By 1894, the strongly nationalistic and Catholic Polish writer Henryk Sienkiewicz had already written a short story about a Roman couple who encountered Jesus on the road to his execution and were healed and converted to his message. Turning his hand to a lengthy treatment of Christians and non-Christians in

Rome in the 60s, Sienkiewicz serialized his book in a Polish magazine, and it would be published in book form by 1896. The Polish origin of the book is reflected in the name of its central female character, Lygia, the Latin term for those who lived in what would become Poland. However, as copyright laws were virtually nonexistent in the late nineteenth century, several non-authorized (one might even call them plagiarized or bootlegged) translations of the Polish original appeared in Western Europe and North America. The author's work would eventually be recognized, in the form of a Nobel Prize for Literature in 1905 and, perhaps more significantly, in a plethora of adaptations and imitations.

Scenes from *Quo Vadis?* were filmed as silent productions in 1912 and 1925, and plans were made to produce a lavish new version of the story in the late 1940s. When it appeared in 1951, *Quo Vadis* (shed of its question mark in the official title) would establish the entire genre of the epic Roman film. It repays studying on that basis alone, but the film itself has emerged as a classic in its own right, particularly in respect to its acting performances, Miklos Rozsa's innovative music, and its evocation of the spirit, and in some cases the words, of the extant ancient sources. While *Quo Vadis* covered much of the same ground as Cecil B. DeMille's *The Sign of the Cross* (1932)—down to the Roman general (Marcus Vinicius here, instead of Marcus Superbus) who is converted by the love of a pure Christian maiden (Lygia here, in place of Mercia)—it provided spectacular images, sound, and scenarios that could compete with the television screens beginning to creep into Americans' living rooms.

Most famous today as the producer of *The Wizard of Oz* (1939), Mervyn LeRoy, a cousin of Cecil B. DeMille's original business partner Jesse Lasky, was commissioned to direct this piece, and he was given an enormous budget and the ability to film at Cinecittà, the studios once controlled by the government of Fascist Italy. The most inspired piece of casting was Peter Ustinov, who, at twenty-nine years of age, was nearly the same age as the historical Nero in 64, and he resembled Nero's coin portraits and statues. In his tantrums and rages—and in his deliberately poor singing—Ustinov captures the essence of Tacitus's and Suetonius's image of the emperor.

The signal contributions of the film's composer also lodged the film in popular memory and established the Roman fanfares that can still be heard in virtually every production set in ancient times. Born in Budapest in 1907, Rozsa had emigrated to the U.K. in the 1930s and found his way to Hollywood when World War II began in 1939. When he was commissioned to score the film, he decided, in his own recollection, "to be stylistically, absolutely correct. First, thorough research had to be made." Throughout an article published in 1951's *Film Music Notes,* Rozsa underscored the painstaking work he performed to determine what sorts of instruments, and thus sounds, could have been produced in first-century Rome. Insisting that the music for a historical film had to be "absolutely authentic," "realistic and factual," Rozsa sought out "ancient" melodies wherever possible and even claimed that Nero's opening song was "in Phrygian mode and dates from the first or second century." While most scholars doubt the absolute authenticity of the film score, there is no doubt that the tenor and generic sound of Rozsa's rousing music became the standard for later composers.

Nevertheless, the employment of an Oxford University–trained historical advisor also secured some degree of authenticity and historical fidelity to the script. Hugh Gray reflected on his experiences in a delightful essay entitled "When in Rome…," published in 1956's *Hollywood Quarterly*, although he focused more on the work habits and linguistic semantics of the Italian crew than on specific instances of his "advice." Substantial portions of Sienkiewicz's novel were cut for the screen adaptation, and specific elements drawn from Tacitus (*Annals* 15.38–44; 16.18–19) and Suetonius (*Life of Nero*, chapters 38, 41, and 50) enhance the "authenticity" of the piece. Moreover, the film makes subtle and sophisticated allusions to the recent past, particularly linking Nero's despotic regime with contemporary totalitarian regimes. Whether specifically alluding to Fascist Italy, Nazi Germany, and/or the Stalinist Soviet Union, *Quo Vadis* draws attention to the perils of megalomaniacal dictators, a danger all too familiar to audiences in the aftermath of World War II.

Recommended Scenes

➤ After a stirring overture, the film opens on the musical theme of "Quo Vadis, Domine?," and its subject is introduced by a voiceover prologue, spoken by the character Marcus Vinicius, 00:03:16 through 00:06:20. Pay particular attention to the statements and allusions in the prologue, and note especially the adaptation of dying "to make men free" from the American "Battle Hymn of the Republic." What might the references to war and to slavery have meant to American audiences in the 1950s?

➤ A delightful introduction to Nero ensues, as he sings to the "omnivorous power" of the "lampent flame," 00:08:55 through 00:14:15. Gaius (not Titus, as in Tacitus) Petronius is introduced as Nero's cynical "Arbiter of Elegance," and compare Tacitus, *Annals* 16.18.

➤ Vinicius, Petronius's nephew, is accorded a triumph, and Nero is forced to make an appearance before the public even though "they irk me," 00:30:02 through 00:38:10.

➤ While most of the first half of the film chronicles the developing love story between Marcus and Lygia, a group of Christians holds a clandestine meeting, beginning at 01:06:59 through 01:08:50. The idea of meeting at night might have been derived from Pliny the Younger's famous letter to the Emperor Trajan (from the 110s CE) concerning the practices of the "Christians" he encountered in Bithynia.

➤ [The following scenes are found on the second disc, with times beginning again.]

➤ One of the best moments in the film is Nero's unveiling of his plans for a new Rome, 00:02:32 through 00:07:54. Echoing the laughter of Charles Laughton in *The Sign of the Cross*, Ustinov complains about the ugliness of the existing city and declares, "Let it be *wonderful*—or let it be awful! So long as it is *uncommon*!" Some of the lines in the speech seem to be adapted from Suetonius, *Nero* 38, and the model of Rome he unveils has a special, checkered history of its own, as it was originally displayed in the Fascist-era *Mostra Augustea della Romanità*, "Augustan Display of Romanness" in 1937/1938. By 1951, it was housed in the *Museo della Civiltà Romana*, where it remains today, and acute viewers may also have been thinking of the models for a new Berlin, designed by Albert Speer, that mesmerized Hitler in his bunker in early 1945.

➤ Another pivotal series of scenes chronicles the fire spreading through Rome in July 64, 00:09:58 through 00:25:02. The sequence culminates in Nero's quest for a suitable scapegoat, to deflect the (deserved, in this case) rumor that he has set fire to the city in order to replace it with "Neropolis." In a chilling moment, Nero declares that, once he is done with these Christians, "history will not be sure that they ever existed." As the full horror of the Holocaust was beginning to be appreciated in the late 1940s, audiences would surely have seen the parallels between the persecution of Christians and the Nazi attempt to exterminate all of Europe's Jews during the War.

➤ The legend of Peter and "Quo vadis, Domine?" is dramatized, followed by Petronius's suicide and his satirical farewell to Nero, 00:33:50 through 00:44:18. Notice particularly the hilarious insertion of a "weeping vase" in Nero's reaction to the event.

➤ The Christians continue to sing while they are set on fire—the detail of Christians serving as illuminated torches is adapted from Tacitus, *Annals* 15.44—between 00:59:34 and 01:07:08.

➤ The revolt against Nero and his ignominious end are improperly placed here, at 01:11:45 through 01:22:22, instead of four years *after* the Great Fire. However, his murder of

Poppaea (in 65 CE, according to Tacitus *Annals* 16.6) and the presence of his former lover Acte at his death (Suetonius, chapter 50) have some historical basis.

Discussion Questions

1. Should the film be interpreted as a commentary on contemporary totalitarian regimes in the 1940s and 1950s?

2. What are the specific echoes of the Holocaust in this film, and how does the film deal with issues of anti-Semitism?

3. What role does Petronius play in the film, and why does he not convert to Christianity before his suicide?

Further Reading and Viewing

The essential analysis of this film, together with the original novel and a more recent made-for-television adaptation of the story in Poland, is Ruth Scodel and Anja Bettenworth's *Whither Quo Vadis?* (Wiley-Blackwell, 2009). A specialized study of the characterization of Nero in this film and previous ones is provided by Maria Wyke, in "Make like Nero! The appeal of a cinematic emperor," in J. Elsner and J. Masters (eds.), *Reflections of Nero: culture, history, & representation* (University of North Carolina Press, 1994), pp. 11–28.

For an appreciation of the model of "Neropolis" that Nero unveils in the film, see Giuseppina Pisani Sartorio, "Le plan-relief d'Italo Gismondi," in F. Hinard and M. Royo (eds.), *Rome: L'espace urbain et ses représentations* (Presses de l'Université de Paris-Sorbonne, 1991), pp. 257–277.

A superb "making-of" documentary of the film, featuring Maria Wyke among others, can be found on the two-disc special edition DVD of the film released in 2008.

Agora

Film Data

Year: 2009
Director: Alejandro AmenábarWriters: Alejandro Amenábar and Mateo Gil
Historical Advisors: Elisa Garrido and Justin Pollard
Length: 125 minutes
Rating: R

Connection to *The Cultures of the West* by Clifford R. Backman

Chapter 8: "The Early Middle Ages."

Preview

Agora centers on the circumstances leading to the murder of Hypatia, a philosopher, mathematician, and teacher, by a Christian mob in Alexandria (Egypt) in 415 CE. Born around 360 CE and instructed by her father Theon, a mathematician and last librarian of the famous Library at Alexandria, Hypatia directed the Platonic school in the city, teaching students who were of mixed religious commitments but, presumably, all men. The few sources that mention her agree that she was abducted, stripped of her clothes, and stoned to death with roof tiles by a deranged group of Christians, but the precise sequence of events that led to this atrocity has always been controversial. Because all of these sources were composed by Christians—with the exception of her own correspondence with a former student, the Bishop Synesius of Cyrene—the lynching of Hypatia may be interpreted as an instance of fanaticism attempting to destroy reason, or as the elimination of a dangerous pagan influence in the midst of a Christianizing Egypt.

The latter approach has, unfortunately, been more common, given Christian influence—and misogyny—in Western societies and the installation of her main opponent, Bishop Cyril of Alexandria, as one of the "Fathers of the Church." Hypatia was even depicted as a wicked temptress in the 1853 novel *Hypatia, or New Foes with an Old Face* by Charles Kingsley (exponent of "muscular Christianity" in Victorian Britain). A young Spanish filmmaker believed that the story of Hypatia deserved an updated and more sympathetic treatment for a new millennium, and his original idea was to include her story among those who had used reason to advance the cause of science, particularly in respect to astronomy. However, Amenábar soon came to realize that the story of Hypatia could stand alone and still speak to the concerns of Western societies in the early twenty-first century.

Deciding to recount her tale in the English language and commissioning mostly English-speaking actors for the main roles, Amenábar meticulously recreated some of the physical appearance of Alexandria in the late fourth and early fifth centuries CE, while also employing extremely innovative camera techniques and wide-angle shots to tell his story visually. He claimed that he developed his production design, from costumes to hairstyles to the casting of extras, from the famous Fayyum portraits, and he used 3-D digital storyboards and computer graphics to sketch out the main elements of the film. Most interestingly, however, he periodically pulls the camera dramatically away from the action on the ground and focuses upon the stars or upon the planet Earth moving in space. The film also offers several overhead shots of crowds moving quickly, suggesting how minuscule the actions of people might look to any of the "gods" who are being invoked at the moment.

Agora can be used to illustrate one of the most significant transitional moments in Western Civilization, when non-Christian intellectuals were forced to convert to the new faith or shunted aside if they refused. While some of the scientific speculation may be inappropriate—it is unlikely, for instance, that Hypatia formulated the concept of elliptical planetary orbits, some 1,200 years before Kepler—the overall themes of the film are also of critical importance in today's world.

Determined to celebrate the "heroism of those who use reason," the director risked offending religious adherents of all types, from Christians to Jews to Muslims. Conflicts over the proper place of religious expression in secular Western Europe constantly arise in our own time, and issues of gender and education sometimes intersect with these. France's ban on the *niqab* and other overt forms of religious identity in the public "forum" come to mind, but one might also recall the al-Qaeda-inspired bombing of Madrid's central train station in 2004. *Agora* may be suggesting that religion simply provides the excuse for episodes of horrific violence and that scientific progress can be made only when religious dogma is not allowed to interfere.

Recommended Scenes

➢ Captions establish the setting of the film, Alexandria in 391 CE, and a cosmic view of our planet, with the African continent filling most of the frame, is shown. In her school, Hypatia describes the Ptolemaic system of planetary motion (around the earth, with the earth remaining stationary) and his preference for "perfect" circles, 00:00:40 through 00:03:43.

➤ Outraged by the growing numbers of Christian slaves in his household, Hypatia's father Theon beats Davus, and Hypatia tends to his wounds. Clearly in love with his mistress, Davus makes a model of the Ptolemaic system and explains the epicycle theory to the other students, 00:09:10 through 00:15:20.

➤ A violent riot directed by the priest of Serapis against Christians backfires, and the "pagans" are besieged in their temple, which currently houses the remains of the library, between 00:28:13 and 00:35:48.

➤ Negotiations allow the pagans to evacuate the Serapeum, but Hypatia is determined to save as many scrolls from the library as possible before the Christian mob pours into the precinct. The Christians gleefully turn over the library's shelves and rip apart and burn what they consider "pagan filth," 00:46:57 through 00:55:06.

➤ Another wonderful overhead shot introduces Alexandria's harbor, and many years pass (actually over twenty-five, but Rachel Weisz, playing Hypatia, appears not to have aged). Cyril is now installed as the city's bishop, and he advocates violence against Alexandrian Jews, 00:58:50 through 01:03:35.

➤ Reprisals against this violence by Jews result in even more violence in the street, and Hypatia watches in horror as her fellow citizens destroy each other. Here again, the planetary view is given, and the screams of those killed in the violence echo into space, 01:14:02 through 01:20:03.

➤ Cyril quotes from the New Testament book I Timothy to the effect that a woman should not be suffered to instruct men, and then demands to know whether Orestes, newly installed as the city's prefect, agrees with the Bible on this point. Orestes is a former student of Hypatia and still in love with her, even after she rejected his overtures, and so he refuses to commit himself. The monk Ammonius throws a stone at Orestes, and the targeting of Hypatia by Cyril and his followers is becoming ever more clear, 01:29:01through 01:39:35.

➤ In an extremely effective dénouement, Hypatia is confronted with the demand to submit to a public baptism and, after her refusal, is captured by Christians, stripped, and abused. Her former slave Davus suffocates her so that she can avoid the pain of stoning, and then the camera pulls back to heaven's view of this moment, between 01:47:32 and 01:59:33.

Discussion Questions

1. How does the camera movement in the film enhance the plot?

2. What role does the astronomical plot play in the film?

3. Is the film anti-Christian? Does it condemn fanaticism of all types?

Further Reading and Viewing

Due in part to the controversy surrounding it and some attacks on it by Christian groups, *Agora* was not widely released in the United States. However, it earned favorable reviews in some quarters, and among the best is Susan Jacoby's article, "Reason is the Star of *Agora*," http://newsweek.washingtonpost.com/onfaith/spirited_atheist/2010/06/agora_a_rare_movie_with_reason_as_its_star.html. A scholarly treatment of Hypatia can be found in Maria Dzielska's *Hypatia of Alexandria* (Harvard University Press, 1995).

Becket

Film Data

Year: 1964
Director: Peter Glenville
Screenplay: Edward Anhalt
Based on the play *Becket*, by Jean Anouilh
Music: Laurence Rosenthal
Length: 150 minutes
Rating: PG-13

Connection to *The Cultures of the West* by Clifford R. Backman

Chapter 9: "Reform and Renewal, 750–1250"

Chapter 10: "Worlds Brought Down, 1250–1400"

Preview

The story of the murder of Thomas à Becket in his Canterbury cathedral, by a group of knights who may or may not have been sent by King Henry II of England, is a familiar one and has been enacted in many plays and films ever since 1170. Because his shrine became a pilgrimage site—and was the destination of the group of pilgrims immortalized in Chaucer's *Canterbury Tales*, among many others—Becket continued to exert a powerful grip on the English imagination, even after the country was officially converted to Protestantism in the sixteenth century. However, the tale is of more than national interest, since conflicts between church and secular authorities appeared in various forms across Western Europe and repeatedly throughout the Middle Ages.

By the early twentieth century, the crucial matters of dispute in these conflicts, involving simony, investiture, benefices, and ecclesiastical adjudication, began to appear ever more arcane and abstruse. Playwrights opted instead to explore the interior psychology of Becket and his king and the relationship between these two determined individuals. T. S. Eliot's deservedly famous *Murder in the Cathedral* (1935) focused particularly on the doubts and inner conflicts within Becket, who wonders whether he is doing "the right deed for the wrong reason," and he even offered the four murderous knights the chance to justify their actions, directly to the audience.

While Eliot dealt with wider issues of church vs. state and the degree to which God's directives are knowable, Jean Anouilh centered his version of the story on the thwarted friendship between the two men, and he introduced interesting, if incorrect elements of race and collaboration in the process. The play, *Becket, ou l'Honneur de Dieu* (*Becket, or The Honor of God)* was first produced in Paris in 1959 and then translated into English for an American stage production in 1960. Anouilh claimed that he was first drawn to the Becket legend when he bought a book on the Norman Conquest of England—mainly because its green binding had caught his eye in a bookstand along the Seine.

Furthermore, Anouilh cheerfully admitted that he had constructed Becket as a Saxon, i.e., a member of the "race" conquered by the Normans beginning in 1066, a situation that historians have concluded is impossible. Nevertheless, the unlikely friendship between a Norman king and a Saxon churchman became the hinge upon which the play turns, as Becket rediscovers his piety and his Saxon identity, determined to oppose the king and his Norman occupiers. It is not difficult to imagine the contemporary resonance for a play of this type, in a Paris that had suffered the humiliation of occupation by a foreign power—and the pressure to collaborate with representatives of that power—in its very recent past.

The original New York production had boasted Laurence Olivier in the title role and Anthony Quinn as Henry II, but, when a film adaptation was proposed, director Peter Glenville cast Richard Burton and Peter O'Toole. The boisterous performances of both men were instrumental to the success of the film, as was its music, chosen and interwoven like a medieval tapestry by Laurence Rosenthal. The score incorporates both medieval church music and short Welsh songs, in Welsh, as it attempts to recreate the tension between occupiers and occupied in twelfth-century England. The film was a critical and commercial success, and O'Toole was asked to reprise his role as Henry II in the 1968 adaptation of James Goldman's play *The Lion in Winter.* (In this case, though, the colorless and nagging Eleanor of Aquitaine of *Becket* was replaced by the inimitable Katharine Hepburn, who received her third of four Academy Awards for the performance.)

Recommended Scenes

- ➤ *Becket* opens with King Henry II submitting to humiliation over Becket's tomb in penance for his murder, 00:01:56 through 00:07:01. From the beginning, the theme of racial conflict is invoked, as Henry complains about the pleasure the penance will give to "these treacherous Saxon monks of yours."

- ➤ Most of the rest of the film is Henry's recollection of his relationship with Thomas, from their boys-will-be-boys period through the conflict that resulted in Thomas's murder. (Anouilh had envisioned this more as a conversation between Henry and Thomas's spirit in the cathedral, but this device was dispensed with for the film.)

- ➤ There are hints of the later conflict when priests complain to Henry about their being taxed and about the necessity of priests being tried by ecclesiastical (church) courts rather than by the secular (state, controlled by the king) courts. Henry complains in his turn about their "unpriestly caterwauling" about money, 00:13:20 through 00:21:10.

- ➤ Becket wonders aloud about his own personal honor, when he is now collaborating with the Norman conqueror as Henry's chancellor. A Saxon monk fails to assassinate him, but this man will become a trusted associate of Becket until his final moments, 00:40:32 through 00:45:06.

- ➤ Henry unexpectedly appoints Becket archbishop, because he wants "his man" in the office, 00:53:37 through 01:03:26. Contrary to expectations, Becket takes the position seriously and humbles himself through acts of charity—all while wearing his archbishop's ring on the same hand as his chancellor's ring.

- ➤ The issue of the trial of a churchman by ecclesiastical or secular courts is finally raised, and the relationship between the king and his bishop rapidly deteriorates. The film employs a simple "two-shot" of Becket and Henry debating the points of the issue, but all the while the friendship between the men is the real concern, 01:19:12 through 01:22:39.

- ➤ Worldly, realistic cardinals in Rome—complete with Italian accents—complain about Becket's having "too much sincerity," and the pope protests that he wishes the church to exist peacefully within the state, 01:49:25 through 01:54:50.

> ➤ After a night of binge drinking with four Norman knights, the king asks his fateful question, "Will no one rid me of this meddlesome priest?" and the knights steal out to kill Becket, 02:10:13 through 02:15:12.

> ➤ The murder of Becket is graphically depicted, complete with torn vestments under a hail of sword thrusts, and the scene returns to Henry's penance over Becket's stony countenance, between 02:19:35 and 02:27:54.

Discussion Questions

1. Does *Becket* obscure the nature of the central power struggle between Henry II and Thomas Becket?

2. How and why is the theme of collaboration with an occupier introduced in the film?

3. Does the film include a homoerotic element in the friendship between Thomas and Henry?

Further Reading and Viewing

A tie-in book, including a translation of Anouilh's play by Lucienne Hill and an introduction by Anouilh, was published by the New American Library in 1964, and a French version of the play—with a cover image inspired by the film—was published by Le Livre de Poche (Paris, 1967). A new biography of Becket by John Guy, entitled *Thomas Becket: Warrior, Priest, Rebel; A Nine-Hundred-Year-Old Story, Retold* (Random House), appeared in 2012.

Recollecting his fascination with ancient Rome in the press-book, *Gladiator: The Making of the Ridley Scott Epic* (Newmarket Press, 2000, p. 26), Scott had observed, "Because what I love to do—apart from getting a good script and making movies—where I enjoy myself most, I think, is creating worlds. Sometimes new worlds, i.e. science fiction, or recreating a world that's historical." While scholars have generally doubted that he achieved the aim of "historical accuracy" in *Kingdom of Heaven*, the themes raised in the film are obviously pertinent ones in the first decades of the present millennium.

Recommended Scenes

➤ The dying father of young Balian (played by Orlando Bloom, even though the historical Balian was in his forties in this period) imparts his vision of a peaceful future between Muslims and Christians, 00:20:41 through 00:24:20. Balian notices that Muslim prayers "sound like our prayers," and his more ecumenical sensibility is contrasted with the fanatical Guy de Lusignan, who deplores Christian friendships with Muslims.

➤ A Crusader assault on a Muslim caravan occasions an argument over "what God wills," 00:58:20 through 01:01:45.

➤ Guy de Lusignan longs for a war with Saladin, and Reynald de Châtillon provides the excuse by capturing Saladin's sister. Guy kills Saladin's emissary and war breaks out, between 01:27:00 and 01:29:58.

➤ The defeat of the Crusaders at Hattin is impressively depicted—with circling vultures over the dusty landscape—and Balian prepares to defend Jerusalem. In a crucial, if implausible, speech, Balian insists that Jerusalem's inhabitants matter more than its holy places, 01:36:44 through 01:58:52.

➤ Having defended his city as well as he could (in a thrilling series of scenes depicting medieval siege warfare), Balian surrenders for terms, and encounters Saladin in the flesh. In a brief but memorable performance by Ghassan Massoud, Saladin declares that, because he is Saladin, Balian can trust him. Each man recognizes the inherent nobility in the other, and each seems doubtful as to the intrinsic worth of the holy places in the city that is ostensibly sacred to both faiths, 02:04:22 through 02:07:38.

Discussion Questions

1. Is the notion of a "kingdom of heaven" at all realistic, given the endemic religious violence of the twelfth century?

2. Is the portrait of Saladin in *Kingdom of Heaven* consistent with his image, at least in the Christian West of the Middle Ages?

3. Is Scott pointing the way to a resolution of conflict in the modern Middle East by means of this film?

Further Reading and Viewing

Saladin's conquest of Jerusalem is probably best examined from the perspective of Arab chroniclers. A collection of reactions to this event, compiled from Arabic sources, may be found in Francesco Gabrieli's *Arab Historians of the Crusades*, translated by E. J. Costello (Routledge & Kegan Paul, 1969), Part Two: "Saladin and the Third Crusade." A biography of Saladin by Anne-Marie Eddé, translated by Jane Marie Todd, has recently been published by Harvard University Press (2011).

On *Kingdom of Heaven* in particular, one might consult an essay by Simona Slanička, "*Kingdom of Heaven*: Der Kreuzzug Ridley Scotts gegen den Irakkrieg" ("*Kingdom of Heaven*: Ridley Scott's Crusade against the War in Iraq"), in M. Meier and S. Slanička (eds.), *Antike und Mittelalter im Film: Konstruktion—Dokumentation—Projektion* (Köln: Böhlau Verlag, 2007), pp. 385–397.

Jungfrukällan (The Virgin Spring)

Film Data

Year: 1960
Director: Ingmar Bergman
Cinematographer: Sven Nykvist
Screenplay: Ulla Isaksson
Based on a thirteenth-century Swedish ballad
Length: 89 minutes
Rating: No rating

Connection to *The Cultures of the West* by Clifford R. Backman

Chapter 8: "The Early Middle Ages."

Preview

Delving again into the medieval world he had explored so memorably in *The Seventh Seal* (1957), Bergman turned to a well-known legend of violence, revenge, and atonement, while adding a historical element of religious transformation. Ulla Isaksson adapted the story of the film from a thirteenth-century Swedish ballad entitled "Töres dotter i Vänge" ("Töre's Daughter at Vänge"). As she described the process, Isaksson fleshed out the characters of the parents, whose beloved daughter is raped and murdered by a gang of three bandits, while also adding characters and scenes that would underscore the historical relevance of the story. Although Sweden had technically been converted to Christianity several centuries earlier, elements of the older, pre-Christian religion were still visible in the thirteenth century, and Isaksson incorporated the theme of revenge within a pre-Christian warrior code.

Although the parents of the murdered child have converted to Christianity in the story—and the mother is conspicuously pious—they number among their household a foster daughter, Ingeri, who prays to Odin and cloaks her resentment of Karin, the beautiful, blonde center of the household, in religious terms. When Töre and Märeta discover that the three men they are sheltering in their home—as an act of Christian charity—have violated and murdered their child, they do not hesitate to exact a terrible vengeance. Töre assumes the uniform, sword, and attitude of a pre-Christian warrior, ritually preparing himself for the execution by knocking over a tree, collecting its branches, and beating himself with them as he bathes. He wakes up the older men and kills them efficiently and pitilessly, and then he turns attention to the third, a young boy who witnessed the rape and murder but did not actively participate. Töre heaves the child up and dashes him to the ground, and, while Märeta can feel some sympathy for the boy, they have both decided that retributive violence is the only way to rectify the horrific violation of their daughter.

The Virgin Spring is deservedly considered a classic of world cinema, and it is important to realize how daring and controversial it appeared in 1960, when it was first released. The film unsparingly depicted the forcible rape of a young girl by two men, followed by her violent murder, and it did not flinch from a graphic depiction of the execution of the three criminals. It also employed an innovative technique by having Töre pour out his grief to God, in long-shot and with his back to the camera, when he finds Karin's body in the forest. While the purity of the girl is acknowledged by a spring that flows from where her head had rested, the complicity of God in witnessing violence and not halting it is explored in all its complexity here.

Recommended Scenes

➤ A Christian man and woman prepare their virginal daughter Karin to make a long journey to church, deputing her to carry an offering of candles for the Virgin Mary, 00:11:47 through 00:18:08. The opening scenes stress the relatively high status of the family, but there is also an undercurrent of resentment for this Christianization among some members of the household.

➤ A pregnant Ingeri, terrified of going into the woods, stays with a pagan hermit at the verge of the forest, while her mistress goes on alone. Karin is lured off the path by three men, and, in her innocence and inability to see their true intentions, finds herself in an extremely dangerous situation. The men subdue and violently rape her, and then, after she moans in grief, one of them beats her to death, 00:30:47 through 00:44:12.

➤ The murderers inadvertently seek shelter at the home of the murdered girl's parents, and, in a fatal mistake, they try to sell the beautiful—and unique—dress worn by Karin to her mother. Märeta locks the door on the barn where they are sleeping and informs her husband of the situation, between 01:01:28 and 01:12:20.

➤ Töre steals in on the criminals while they sleep, waits for them to wake up, and then ritually slaughters all three, including the boy, 01:16:09 through 01:21:11.

➤ Töre, Märeta, Ingeri, and the other members of the household find Karin's body, and Töre expresses his grief and bewilderment against God, 01:24:19 through 01:29:05. A fountain appears under Karin's head, and Ingeri baptizes her face in the water.

Discussion Questions

1. How does the film underscore the complex relationship between Christian and "pagan" forms of worship in the Middle Ages?

2. How is the theme of vengeance connected to the theme of pagan/Christian interaction?

3. How does the film deal with issues of gender and sexuality in the Middle Ages?

Further Reading and Viewing

The Criterion edition of *The Virgin Spring*, released in 2006, contains an introduction by filmmaker Ang Lee, new interviews with the film's younger actresses, and audio commentary by Bergman on the craft of filmmaking. An included booklet features essays on the film and a commentary by Ulla Isaksson on how she adapted the medieval ballad into a workable screenplay.

The Name of the Rose

Film Data

Year: 1986
Director: Jean-Jacques Annaud
Based on the novel by Umberto Eco
Production Design: Dante Ferretti
Music: James Horner
Length: 131 minutes
Rating: R

Connection to *The Cultures of the West* by Clifford R. Backman

Chapter 10: "Worlds Brought Down, 1250–1400"

Preview

This film is described in its opening titles as a "palimpsest" (a manuscript that has been reused) of the delightful 1980 novel of the same name by Umberto Eco. In addition to being a prolific novelist, Eco is also a professor of semiotics at the Università di Bologna, and there is a sly reference in the film to a manuscript containing the annotations of an "Umberto di Bologna." Such quick and witty allusions are a hallmark of Eco's style, and *The Name of the Rose* was far more than a conventional murder mystery set in the Middle Ages. Even the title of the book hints at Eco's professional fascination with words and their meaning, since the full sentence referred to is, "All that remains of a dead rose is the name." (The quote is drawn from a twelfth-century Benedictine monk's poem *De contemptu mundi*, "On Contempt for the World.")

In an interview about the film in the 1980s, Eco observed that his novel—though set in a northern Italian monastery in 1327—addressed a "time of uncertainty" that was very much like our own time. The world, and particularly the intellectual world, was undergoing a profound transition, and Eco diagnosed this transition as one out of blind faith (literally, in that its main exponent is the blind monk Jorge) and into logic, reason, and the erasure of superstition. Eco named the novel's hero and primary investigator of the mystery William of Baskerville, and the Sherlock Holmesian allusions are carried to their logical extension when

William actually comments to his Watson-like assistant monk, "Elementary, my dear Adso." As Conan Doyle's great detective had pursued logic and reason wherever they led in his investigations, Eco suggested that a similarly incisive mind could have solved murders nearly six hundred years earlier. Such a man would, in all probability, have been associated with the institutional church, and yet, because he attributed the deaths to human agency rather than to supernatural forces, he might have been considered a heretic by his more fanatical contemporaries.

A multinational European production, headed by the French director Annaud, attempted to bring the novel to the screen, and Eco praised Annaud's team for "creating a world around the mystery" he had sketched out. Consulting with the famous medievalist Jacques Le Goff, Annaud strove for historical authenticity in *tous les éléments matériels*, "all the material elements," as Le Goff commented. In the film, the Middle Ages itself became a character, and elaborate sets were constructed outside Rome, at Cinecittà, and at Eberbach near the German Rhine. An international cast, headed by Sean Connery as William, was assembled, and filming went on briskly and efficiently as the body count mounted up onscreen. A satisfying conclusion of the mystery wraps up the details of the murders, but William's identification of the killer leads to a fire in the monastery that destroys untold numbers of priceless manuscripts in its secret library. Such accidents must have resulted in real losses for all of us, and Annaud may have been implying that cultural progress is fragile and remains similarly at risk in today's world.

Recommended Scenes

➤ The Franciscan friar William of Baskerville and his assistant Adso have come to an Italian monastery in order to attend a debate, set against the backdrop of tension between the emperor and the pope (this monastery owes allegiance to the pope in Avignon, a reference to the "Babylonian Captivity" of the church).

➤ When he arrives, the Abbot informs William of a problem that has befallen his monastery in recent days, the unsolved mystery surrounding the death of a young manuscript illuminator. The scene also introduces the element of diabolical influence and the forces of religious fundamentalism, between 00:08:22 through 00:15:33.

➤ While William pursues his investigations into the death, measuring footprints and looking for clues, two more deaths occur, and these seem more likely to be murders. The discovery of the victims' blackened fingers and tongues suggests a connection between the monks' habit of licking their fingers while reading and their deaths. Accordingly, reading—at least when the books are poisoned—can literally be deadly, as developed between 01:00:10 and 01:06:15.

➤ William and Adso discover the fantastic and stuffed secret library in the monastery, and William exults in the number of books, generally considered lost, that are available in the library stacks, 01:13:08 through 01:20:45.

➤ Papal envoys arrive, and a debate commences about whether Jesus owned his own cloak. The debate is—and is designed to be—esoteric in the extreme, but there is a serious issue at its heart. This is essentially whether the church itself should have possessions or renounce them and adopt a lifestyle of poverty, as the Franciscans officially had. In the midst of this debate another monk is murdered, 01:30:55 through 01:34:54.

➤ The murderer is unveiled, and he insists that the murders were justified, in order to prevent the dissemination of unholy knowledge. A fire in the library results in the destruction of even more learning, but William manages to save a few volumes before exiting the building, 01:47:33 through 02:04:46.

Discussion Questions

1. How does the theme of ecclesiastical poverty relate to the lives of the impoverished peasants who live around the monastery?

2. To what extent was knowledge considered dangerous in the Middle Ages? What sort of knowledge?

3. What role does laughter have in the use of reason? Why is Jorge so opposed to it, whether literally indulged in the scriptorium or justified in the library's books?

Further Reading and Viewing

The 2004 DVD release of the film includes a West German documentary on its production, entitled "*Die Abtei des Verbrechens*," "The Abbey of Crime." Produced in 1986, this short film contains the expected behind-the-scenes footage, but it focuses primarily on the novelist Eco, the director Jean-Jacques Annaud, and the script advisor, historian Jacques Le Goff. Those curious about Eco's style and method should also consult the original novel, together with his many other novels, including *Foucault's Pendulum* (1988) and his most recent *The Prague Cemetery* (2010). The latter is a novelistic treatment of the actual characters involved in the creation of the deadly "Protocols of the Elders of Zion."

Luther

Film Data

Year: 2003
Director: Eric Till
Length: 144 minutes
Rating: PG-13

Connection to *The Cultures of the West* by Clifford R. Backman

Chapter 11: "Renaissances and Reformations, 1350–1550"

Preview

Luther belongs to the genre of "biopic," and, true to its form, it generally omits the more unsavory and controversial elements in Martin Luther's biography. Among the funders of the film, mentioned in the closing credits, were Thrivent Financial for Lutherans and the "Protestant Church of Germany, EKD" (an acronym for the *Evangelische Kirche in Deutschland*). Casting an attractive, young Joseph Fiennes in the title role was only part of a larger strategy of celebrating Luther's life and achievements, while making short work of his often violent outbursts. Although Luther lived a long life and wrote so much that his fingers were, at his death, locked into place around a pen, the film focuses primarily on the early years of his career, and particularly the circumstances that led to his confrontation with the institutional church in the years 1517 through 1520.

Omitted from the film are Luther's debates with other Protestant reformers like Ulrich Zwingli and, significantly, the virulently anti-Semitic tracts that date from the latter years of his life. The most interesting reconfiguration of the actual Luther for the film concerns his role in the famous Peasants' War of the 1520s. Inspired by what they took to be Luther's ideas of revolution against authority, hundreds of thousands of peasants in southern German territories revolted against their lords, and Luther, far from sympathizing with their cause and their grievances, advised the lords to "smite, slay, and stab" the rebels.

Composing a tract entitled *Auch wider die räuberischen und mörderischen Rotten der anderen Bauern* (*Against the Robbing and Murdering Hordes of Peasants*) in 1525, Luther sided with the temporal powers of his age—one of whom, Frederick of Saxony, had literally saved his life by abducting him after the Diet of Worms. The film suggests that Luther had no direct role in the murders of peasants, and he is bewildered when told of the "butchery" that has been inflicted on them. One of Martin's associates confidentially whispers, "Have a care, Martin. You may have need of these butchers," but the scene then moves quickly to an encounter with a runaway nun that will result in Luther's marriage to Katharina von Bora.

Throughout the film, the contemporary resonances of Luther's story are stressed, and the attempt is made to render Luther's story applicable to today's social problems. In the research for his role as the indulgence seller Johann Tetzel, Alfred Molina claimed to have studied American television preachers, and the "hellfire and brimstone" nature of his sermon to the masses may be more a product of the twenty-first than the sixteenth century. However, he does quote the famous jingle "When the coin in the coffer rings, the soul from purgatory springs," and the gullibility of the mob—including a poor woman with a disabled child whom Luther befriends—is given particular attention in the scene. The application of Luther's ideas to socioeconomic inequality is addressed repeatedly in the film, suggesting a role for Christians in the alleviation of poverty. This may, however, be more a contemporary reaction than a reflection of the historical Reformation.

Recommended Scenes

➤ The best scenes in the film are to be found in its opening sequences, which attempt to account for young Luther's ongoing spiritual quest and its ultimate result at Wittenberg, 00:01:40 through 00:13:18. Luther vows to become a monk, if his life is preserved during a thunderstorm, but then he fumbles a mass attended by his hard-hearted and dismissive father, undergoes spiritual torments with the gentle reproofs of his spiritual father Johann von Staupitz, and is bitterly disappointed by the commercialization of religion he discovers in Rome in 1510. All of these events, though fictionalized and amplified, are known from Luther's recollections of his own early life.

➤ The film does not provide an in-depth examination of the renowned, if controversial, "Tower Experience" that preceded Luther's decision to challenge the selling of papal indulgences, but it does attempt to account for his turn away from the institutional church, 00:21:55 through 00:26:03.

➤ Tetzel makes his fiery appeal to a Wittenberg crowd, and Luther flares up in anger at the exploitation of the poor people of his town by the indulgence sellers, between 00:31:50 and 00:41:46.

➤ After his Ninety-Five Theses reverberate (literally) through the church, Pope Leo X issues his bull of excommunication *Exsurge, Domine*, "Rise up, Lord" in 1520, 01:00:33 through 01:06:06. *Luther* incorporates a very clever image in this scene, having Leo hunt an actual boar while describing Luther as an *aper de silva*, a "boar from the forest" that is trampling God's vineyard.

➤ Luther makes his stand at Worms, is removed for his safety to the Wartburg, and presses on with the difficult work of translating the Bible into German. As a result, he acknowledges he is "turning the world upside down," although Fiennes's Luther claims he never intended the butchery that has resulted from the Peasants' War, 01:17:53 through 01:37:30.

➤ "Religious freedom" is established by the Peace of Augsburg in 1530, and the captions point to Luther's lasting influence in terms of religion, language, and culture, 01:51:12 through 01:55:38.

Discussion Questions

1. Does the film suggest that Luther, particularly in his youth, was psychologically disturbed?

2. Does *Luther* suggest that Martin was, himself, responsible for the violent suppression of peasants in the 1520s?

3. How is Luther's theological revolution connected, at least in the film, to the exploitation of the poor in his society? Luther is outraged by the exploitation of the

Further Reading and Viewing

The classic "psycho-historical" analysis of Luther's early life can be found in Erik H. Erikson's *Young Man Luther: A Study in Psychoanalysis and History* (W.W. Norton, 1958), and a good corrective to the tone and contentions in the film can be found in Mark U. Edwards, Jr.'s *Luther's Last Battles: Politics and Polemics, 1531–46* (Fortress Press, 1983).

Elizabeth

Film Data

Year: 1998
Director: Shekhar Kapur
Screenplay: Michael Hirst
Length: 124 minutes
Rating: R

Connection to *The Cultures of the West* by Clifford R. Backman

Chapter 12: "The Last Crusades, 1492–1648"

Preview

The late 1990s witnessed a revival of interest in the historical legacy of England's "Virgin Queen," Elizabeth I, and particularly in film. Elizabeth appeared as a character in 1998's *Shakespeare in Love,* and she was given a star turn by the actress Cate Blanchett in Shekhar Kapur's 1998 "biopic." Recognizing the appearance of two films concerning Elizabeth among the Best Picture nominees, Whoopi Goldberg, the comedian who hosted that year's Academy Awards program, first appeared to the audience in full Elizabethan regalia, complete with forbidding white makeup. However, Kapur claimed that his real interest in Elizabeth was in the making of precisely this iconic image, and specifically how Elizabeth's personality and interior life drove her to present herself in this fashion.

Kapur offered in this film an interpretation of Elizabeth's personality, rather than an in-depth exploration of the international and religious tensions of her era. In order to explain her embrace of official virginity, Kapur dramatizes Elizabeth's relationship with Robert Dudley, the man whose name she spoke in her final moments in 1603 and whose "last letter" was found carefully stored in her jewelry box after her death. Nevertheless, because the film focuses on the early years of her reign and on the final years of her predecessor and half-sister, Mary Tudor, *Elizabeth* necessarily addresses themes of religious violence and tolerance. After an impressive opening titles sequence, laying out the religious conflicts occasioned by Henry VIII's break with the church and the eventual succession of his Catholic daughter Mary to the throne, the film vividly depicts the burning of the stake of three Protestant "heretics." Elizabeth manages to survive all the calls for her execution by an increasingly unstable and panicky Mary to become a competent, moderately minded leader in her own right.

However, *Elizabeth* also makes dramatic use of the challenges Elizabeth faced in 1558 and 1559, as a young woman attempting to navigate the troubled waters of religious intolerance. The England she inherited was in a precarious, weak position in relation to the major powers of her day, primarily Spain and France, and she also faced a worrying border conflict and a rival claimant in Scotland. Kapur's Elizabeth rejects the love of Dudley (whom she "discovers" is already married—the actual situation of Dudley and his wife's mysterious death are not explored here) and puts her country ahead of her personal interests. The real Elizabeth would execute as many Catholics as "Bloody Mary" had Protestants though, admittedly, she would do so over a period of forty-five, as opposed to Mary's five, years.

One could say that Elizabeth was simply lucky enough to live a long life and survive the multiple threats and assassination attempts—as well as the challenges to her reign by Mary Stuart of Scotland and the Spanish Armada in the 1580s. Nonetheless, the film rightly points to the "middle path" Elizabeth chose to steer, between the extremes of Protestantism and Catholicism, that eventually ensured a remarkable degree of peace for her subjects. Other countries would take longer to decide that the interests of the state, and one that would be as neutral as possible in regard to religious matters, should trump the interests of religious orthodoxy. Elizabeth deserves credit for realizing that "the small question of religion," as she protests during her interrogation in Mary's reign, should yield to more weighty matters in the real world.

Recommended Scenes

➤ The opening captions set the scene of religious conflict in England in the 1550s, and an extremely effective and harrowing scene of the execution of three Protestants, two men and a woman, illustrates the actual consequences of this conflict, 00:01:00 through 00:04:36. The film contrasts the gloom and obscurantism of Mary's court with the brightness and frivolity of Elizabeth's entourage.

➤ Elizabeth is brought into the Tower and interrogated by Mary's agents concerning her involvement in a plot against her sister, 00:11:46 through 00:19:43. The film suggests Elizabeth was completely unaware of the plot, and yet she does not bow to Mary's insistence that Catholicism be strengthened in the country, should Elizabeth succeed.

Elizabeth promises merely to act according to the dictates of her conscience, but Mary continues to resist the pressure of her advisors to have Elizabeth killed.

➤ News of Elizabeth's accession arrives, and she is bathed in golden light as she offers a Biblical quote (a moment that is verified by historical records), 00:27:41 through 00:31:03.

➤ Elizabeth enters into an ill-advised war with Marie de Guise, the mother of Mary Stuart of Scotland (and one-time queen of France), 00:41:58 through 00:49:31. The film is not reliable on this point, since Marie de Guise was actually defeated by English forces and Scottish Protestants in 1560. However, the film underscores international doubts about Elizabeth's claim to the throne, and it features a luminous performance by the French actress Fanny Ardant.

➤ The key moment in the film concerns the passage of the Acts of Supremacy and Uniformity in 1559, between 00:52:24 and 00:58:35. Elizabeth maneuvers a middle path over the heads of all the men in her Parliament, and she pledges not to "make windows into men's souls."

➤ Declaring that she will "have one mistress here and no master," Elizabeth rejects her lover Dudley and receives word soon after of her excommunication by the pope, 01:20:02 through 01:25:01. The details are very muddled here, since the pope did not issue this declaration—which effectively authorized any good Catholic to murder the queen—until 1570.

➤ In a scene that rivals—and is probably inspired by--the finale of *The Godfather* (1972),Elizabeth liquidates her opposition, under the calm guidance of Sir Francis Walsingham, her famous "spymaster." The queen prays as her enemies are taken off, including the Duke of Norfolk (in point of fact her cousin, who was not executed until 1572). The idea of reincarnating herself as a Virgin Mary type is developed and implemented, 01:46:52 through 01:54:08.

Discussion Questions

1. Is Elizabeth driven to become ruthless by Walsingham? What are her essential motives?

2. What seem to have been Elizabeth's real attitudes toward religion, at least as implied by the film?

3. Does the film suggest that rule was more difficult for a woman in this period? Why?

Further Reading and Viewing

A re-evaluation of the reign of the Mary Tudor has been undertaken in recent years, and the best example of this is probably Eamon Duffy's *Fires of Faith: Catholic England under Mary Tudor* (Yale University Press, 2009). For a superior, though much longer and more detailed, retelling of Elizabeth's life story, see the six-part 1971 BBC television production *Elizabeth R*, which features Glenda Jackson in the title role.

Ivan the Terrible, Part I

Film Data

Year: 1944
Director: Sergei Eisenstein
Music: Sergei Prokofiev
Length: 103 minutes
Rating: No rating

Connection to *The Cultures of the West* by Clifford R. Backman

Chapter 12: "The Last Crusades, 1492–1648"

Preview

Along with the other major filmmakers of the USSR, Eisenstein was removed to Kazakhstan for the duration of the Second World War and, in the final project of his life, undertook a three-part examination of the life of the Tsar Ivan IV (reigned 1547–1584). Joseph Stalin had often expressed his admiration for *Ivan Grozny*, Ivan the Terrible, who had united a weak and divided Russia, conquered huge swaths of territory, and, perhaps most importantly, dominated the hereditary aristocrats, the boyars, with sheer determination and periodic bouts of violence. Eisenstein would, unfortunately, come to experience some of these fits of temper himself. While Stalin enthusiastically welcomed the first part of the film, released in 1944, he was less satisfied with the second part, which was completed in 1946 but banned in the Soviet Union. In fact, *Ivan the Terrible, Part II* would not be shown in the USSR until 1958, five years after Stalin's death and ten years after Eisenstein had succumbed to a heart attack.

Stalin seems to have been outraged by the suggestion that the *Oprichnina*, Ivan's secret police, could be compared with the Soviet terror apparatus. Eisenstein was brought to the Kremlin and told Stalin's opinion: "Ivan the Terrible was very cruel," he said, "You can depict him as a cruel man, but you have to show why he had to be so cruel." The handsome, noble, and imaginative Ivan of Part I seemed to be replaced by a more ruthless dictator, surrounded by a degenerate and needlessly violent court. The film may thus reflect much of its immediate surroundings, but it also offers a meditation on Russian history, from the perspective of its most prominent filmmaker.

Eisenstein had already produced landmark films recognized around the world for their innovative qualities, such as *Battleship Potemkin* (1925) and *Alexander Nevsky* (1938). The camera angles, wide, staring eyes, elongated shadows, and, above all, the stirring music of Sergei Prokofiev still render Eisenstein's unfinished final film a riveting piece. From the perspective of the historian, they remind Westerners that Russia is also part of the history of Western civilization and that Ivan knew of—and mentions at various moments—Western European monarchs like Elizabeth I of England.

Recommended Scenes

➤ The opening captions praise Ivan as the man who united and created Russia, welding it into a "mighty state" that stretched across vast territories. The scene details the crowning of the Muscovy Prince Ivan in 1547, at seventeen years of age, as Tsar of All the Russias, and he unveils his plans to create a "Third Rome" in Moscow, 00:01:30 through 00:13:10.

➤ The new Tsar fends off a threatened popular revolt, and he unites them into a common cause against the "alien people" in Kazan, 00:21:55 through 00:29:30.

➤ The central element of the film chronicles the siege of Kazan, and Kazakh and Tatar extras accentuate the "reality" of the scene, 00:36:01 through 00:40:54.

➤ The boyars, led by Ivan's diabolical aunt Efrosinia Staritskaya, continue to challenge his authority, and Ivan declares that they are worse than any foreign enemy Russia faces, 01:12:22 through 01:20:37.

➤ Efrosinia manages to have Ivan's wife poisoned, but the people rally to his side and his goal of installing a "Third Rome" is beginning to be realized, between 01:32:14 and 01:38:54.

Discussion Questions

1. How does Ivan's style of government, at least as presented here, compare with those of other contemporaneous monarchs, including Elizabeth I?

2. What does the siege of Kazan, as depicted here, reflect about Soviet attitudes toward its own ethnic minorities?

3. Is Ivan explicitly compared to Stalin in the film?

Further Reading and Viewing

A Criterion Collection version of Parts I and II was released in 2001, together with an essay by J. Hoberman and documentaries on Eisenstein and his legacy.

La Reine Margot (Queen Margot)

Film Data

Year: 1994
Director: Patrice Chéreau
Screenplay: Danièle Thompson and Patrice Chéreau
Music: Goran Bregovic
Length: 144 minutes
Rating: R

Connection to *The Cultures of the West* by Clifford R. Backman

Chapter 12: "The Last Crusades, 1492–1648"

Preview

The St. Bartholomew's Day Massacre, launched on August 23, 1572, was a watershed and emblematic moment in the French Wars of Religion. This series of violent attacks and reprisals began in 1562 and killed tens of thousands of Catholics and Huguenots (French Calvinists) until Henri IV Bourbon declared that *"Paris vaut bien une messe,"* "Paris is worth a mass" and issued the Edict of Nantes in 1598. The murder of roughly two thousand Protestants in a Paris that was still celebrating the marriage of the Catholic princess Marguerite de Valois to the Protestant Henri de Navarre triggered even more violence outside the capital for the next several weeks.

The image of thousands of rotting corpses in the August heat was an inescapable one for playwrights, painters, novelists, and, eventually, filmmakers. Christopher Marlowe produced his *The Massacre at Paris* in 1593, commenting obliquely on how differently matters stood in England in this period, and D. W. Griffith in his influential silent film *Intolerance* (1916) would profile the massacre as one of four historical incidents of intolerance in action. However, the strongest artistic statement on the massacre remains the novel *La Reine Margot*, *Queen Margot*, published by Alexandre Dumas père in 1845. The novel conflates several historical characters and creates an improbable romance between the Princess Marguerite (Margot) and a Protestant whose life she saves on that fateful night, but at its core there is a compelling plea for religious tolerance and understanding.

In the 1990s, Patrice Chéreau decided to revisit the story of this classic novel, perhaps because a call for tolerance across religious divides seemed more relevant than ever. The degree to which Muslim citizens of France are threatened by the Republican tradition of *laïcité* or "secularism" continues to be a matter of debate. Occasionally centered on religious garb, appearance, or language, the debate is connected to wider issues of assimilation, tolerance, and relationships across community lines. By demonstrating the full force of religious violence, accompanied by brutal sixteenth-century weapons and copious amounts of blood, the filmmakers may have hoped to underscore the possible consequences of intolerance in today's world.

The highlight of the film is certainly the fifteen-minute sequence detailing the scope of the massacre, accompanied by powerful music and visceral language. However, the film is brilliantly cast, particularly in its female leads, with Isabelle Adjani as Margot and the Italian actress Virna Lisi as the Queen Mother, Catherine de Medici. Lisi's Italian accent—appropriate for a French queen whose family originated in Florence—is strong and strengthens at moments of tension especially when she shouts at her weak son, Charles IX, and her daughter Margot. The French *besoin*, "need" slips slightly into the Italian *bisogna*, when she explains, echoing Niccolò Macchiavelli (another Florentine), the occasional necessity of swift and brutal action to forestall a worse disaster. *La Reine Margot* draws attention to the fact that Catherine's scheming will only result in the extinction of her family and the succession of the hated "peasant" Henri Bourbon.

Recommended Scenes

➢ Captions explain the religious conflict, ongoing for many years before 1572, and the forced wedding between Marguerite and Henri is depicted in full and often amusing detail, 00:01:55 through 00:10:05.

➢ After an assassination attempt against the Protestant leader Coligny fails, a family conference decides to cover up the evidence by launching a massacre of all Protestants residing in Paris. Against the backdrop of ringing bells, screams, and gunshots, the violent night unfolds, between 00:39:20 and 00:56:46.

➢ Catherine's new son-in-law Henri, even though he is the Huguenot leader of a small independent country, survives the night's horrors, but he is forced to convert—at least nominally—to Catholicism. Margot is still covered with the blood of a man whose life she saved in the palace, 00:57:22 through 01:00:17.

➤ This man, a largely fictional character called La Mole, is left for dead, still clutching a Catholic with whom he had dueled. The public executioner, noticing that the men have been dumped into a common grave but are still alive, rescues them, and the two former enemies become fast and committed friends, 01:17:20 through 01:26:05.

➤ In an innovative twist on the historical record, Charles IX is mistakenly poisoned by a book left for Henri. Charles's mother Catherine is the villainess in the piece, and she has now managed to kill her eldest son, paving the way for the accession of her favorite son as Henri III, 02:00:30 through 02:07:17.

➤ La Mole and his friend Coconnas are executed, but Margot takes La Mole's head with her to exile in Navarre. A Hebrew song closes the film, and captions tell the viewer that her husband Henri will become Henri IV in 1589, 02:14:30 through 02:17:40.

Discussion Questions

1. What motivates the orgy of violence on the night of the massacre?

2. Why does Henri de Navarre convert and reconvert so often?

3. What are the contemporary resonances of the bells rung in August 1572?

Further Reading and Viewing

A superb collection of documents regarding the massacre and its results is available in Barbara B. Diefendorf's *The Saint Bartholomew's Day Massacre: A Brief History with Documents* (Bedford/St. Martin's, 2009). Some of the same territory is covered in the 2010 film *La princesse de Montpensier, The Princess of Montpensier*, which was similarly inspired by a historical novel covering the events of the massacre and in particular its effect on the Guise family.

Vredens Dag (Day of Wrath)

Film Data

Year: 1943
Director: Carl Th. Dreyer
Screenplay: Carl Th. Dreyer
Cinematography: Karl Andersson
Length: 97 minutes
Rating: No rating

Connection to *The Cultures of the West* by Clifford R. Backman

Chapter 12: "The Last Crusades, 1492–1648"

Preview

Vredens Dag is both a masterpiece of world cinema and a thoughtful historical examination of the witch-hunting mania that swept through Europe in the early modern period. Dreyer adapted the film from a 1908 play by the Norwegian playwright Hans Wiers-Jenssen entitled *Anne Pedersdotter, Anne, Peter's Daughter*. The play was inspired by the 1590 burning of an accused witch, the wife of a Lutheran pastor in Bergen, Norway. The subject matter provided for a powerful examination of the psychological forces that led to accusations and to admissions of witchcraft in previous periods.

Dreyer chose to make a film version of this story in the midst of the German occupation of Denmark in World War II. The hiding of a hunted fugitive at the beginning of the film would have had a strong resonance with audiences living under the constant threat of collaboration and reprisals for resistance. As in other periods of intense political pressure, the witchcraft craze was ripe for re-examination, and Dreyer brought the full force of his cinematic talent to the story. Employing sophisticated lighting, tracking his actors with the camera, and focusing particularly on the eyes of the main players, Dreyer made a harrowing story even more intense and compelling to watch. He was also exceptionally fortunate in the actors he cast, especially Lisbeth Movin as Anne, who uses her eyes to gather and exert power over her stepson and her husband. Movin and her co-star, Preben Lerdorff Rye, as her stepson and lover Martin, appeared together under much happier circumstances four decades later, as reunited lovers in the acclaimed *Babette's Feast* (1987).

The film is accompanied by an eerie soundtrack of young boys singing the *Dies Irae*, "Day of Wrath," a thirteenth-century hymn about the Christian Last Judgment. Judgment falls upon many people in the course of the film, but historical judgment of what, precisely, motivated and sustained the witch hunts is also developed here. The complex psychology of Anne, and the statement by Herlof's Marte that "there is power in evil," hint at wider applications of the seemingly bizarre allegations of witchcraft. Simply with the force of her mind and the power of suggestion, Anne causes the death of her hated husband, and the film and play connected the ideas of sexual repression and liberation with religious mania. In the twentieth century as well as in the seventeenth, individuals might declare themselves guilty, with no basis in reality. The irrational mind may remain far more powerful than any rational approach to the world.

Recommended Scenes

➤ In a chilling opening, the song "Day of Wrath" is sung in a minor chord and illustrated with graphic images of destruction from early modern woodcuts, 00:00:20 through 00:04:45. Notice of an accused witch goes out in a document dated 1623, and it appears that Herlof's Marte, the accused, is actually, or behaves suspiciously like, a witch.

➤ Anne, the young wife of the minister Absalon, lives with him and Absalon's mother, a forbidding and judgmental presence in Anne's life. Herlof's Marte comes into Anne's home and begs to be hidden from her pursuers, 00:10:32 through 00:15:57. She hints darkly that Anne owes her this, because she had defended Anne's mother from a similar charge of witchcraft.

➤ Herlof's Marte is captured, interrogated, and tortured. Her naked, elderly body is exposed, and she begs Absalon not to have her burned. When he demurs, she proudly defies him, predicting that his wife Anne will also be denounced as a witch shortly, 00:18:03 through 00:30:14.

➤ The execution scene is horrible to watch, but it employs sophisticated and artistically designed lighting and shadow. Crucifix imagery is seen throughout, and Anne watches the burning in horror through a window, 00:31:03 through 00:35:14.

➤ Anne channels her mother's "power" as a witch and calls her attractive adult stepson Martin to her side. As their affair deepens, they delight in each other, and Anne slyly reads to Martin from the Biblical Song of Solomon about her love, 00:45:28 through 00:51:10.

➤ The crucial scene of the film unfolds between 01:16:30 and 01:19:20. Anne causes Absalon's death through her will and the power of her gaze.

➤ While Absalon's funeral is in progress, his mother accuses Anne of being a witch. Realizing that she has lost Martin's love, Anne confesses and observes that she will be burned, as Herlof's Marte was. The film ends over a reprise of the *Dies Irae* song and the image of a cemetery cross in shadow, 01:27:19 through 01:37:10.

Discussion Questions

1. Is witchcraft real, at least as described in this film?

2. What role did gender and sexuality play in the witchcraft craze, as explored in *Day of Wrath*?

3. How might the film be connected to the historical experience of Denmark in 1943?

Further Reading and Viewing

The 2001 Criterion release of the film contains excerpts of a documentary about Dreyer entitled "My Métier" and interviews from the 1960s and the 1990s with some of the film's actors.

Black Robe

Film Data

Year: 1991
Director: Bruce Beresford
Screenplay: Brian Moore, based on his novel
Length: 101 minutes
Rating: R

Connection to *The Cultures of the West* by Clifford R. Backman

Chapter 13: "Science Breaks Out and Breaks Through"

Preview

Black Robe is a cinematic rendering of Brian Moore's 1985 novel, focusing on the experiences of the Jesuit Father Laforgue in New France (Québec and Ontario) in the 1630s. Father Laforgue feels driven to convert and civilize the native peoples of the St. Lawrence basin, and he encounters widely varying responses to his mission among the Algonquin, Huron, and Iroquois peoples. While the novel is a work of fiction, its basic substance is inspired by specific incidents contained in the famous *Jesuit Relations*, which were published in Paris between 1632 and 1673.

When the French established a fort at what would become Québec City in 1608, they came into contact with established confederations of the native inhabitants, but some Catholic groups in France detected in this incursion into North America a new mission field, ripe for harvest by energetic and very brave young priests. The French had a light and thin administrative presence and were forced to interact and trade with the First Nations peoples surrounding them. North America would later become the scene of bitter colonial struggles between the French, Dutch, and English, but the film focuses particularly on the determination of some to share Christianity with people who had very little interest in giving up their "savage" beliefs.

While there were only two Jesuits in Québec in 1632, thirty to forty would be active in New France by the 1640s. Recruited from Jesuit colleges in France, they were seen as the leading edge of "civilization" in the region, though they were often, as in other parts of the world, subjected to brutal reprisals by native peoples. The level and brutality of the violence directed against them seemed to reinforce, in some minds, the "savagery" that dominated these cultures, and this strengthened calls to continue the missions. The end result of this contact was, as in many regions touched by Europeans, death on an unimaginable scale, due to disease as well as to violent subjugation.

The film, like the novel that inspires it, asks clear and pointed questions about who were the civilized in this historical moment and who the savages. The languages, stories, and religions of the various native peoples are showcased, and their religious officials battle for the hearts and minds of their people with Father Laforgue. In the course of the novel, Laforgue is beaten, has a finger severed by a shell with a sharp edge, and suffers cold, hunger, and abandonment. Nevertheless, at the end of the film, he can declare that he does, after all, love the people of New France and is still committed to sharing Christianity with them.

The story of Laforgue is inspired by many separate accounts in the *Jesuit Relations*, coupled with Moore's superb imagination, but the closest historical parallel is probably Jean de Brébeuf, who was tortured and killed during an Iroquois invasion of Huron territory (in today's southern Ontario) in 1649 and then made a saint in the Catholic Church. Brébeuf had spent many years among the Hurons, learning their language and operating missions among them from 1626 to 1629 and again from 1634 until his murder in 1649. The missions founded among the Hurons were sometimes successful and sometimes abandoned, often due to outbreaks of disease. When influenza killed a great many Hurons in 1637, the Jesuits were suspected of spreading the disease deliberately, through some sort of black magic, and several French people were killed.

Images of Brébeuf with burning axe blades seared into his body, placed alongside pictures of other Jesuits being burned alive or hacked to death with their already-mutilated fingers clasped in prayer, reinforced European notions of the "uncivilized" nature of First Nations peoples. However, this film casts the story differently, asking whether the "Black Robes," the term applied to the priests by the bewildered natives, should have attempted this conversion at all.

Recommended Scenes

➤ The credits open over seventeenth-century maps of the St. Lawrence and Great Lakes region, and the drawings of violence by native people and the identification of a settlement of *sorciers*, magicians, is noted on the map, 00:00:42 through 00:04:22. The date of the film, 1634, is given, together with a sense of the region's recent past.

➤ The French under Samuel de Champlain and the Algonquin prepare for a conference, and the film stresses the similarity of their preparations, as both groups employ clothes, gifts, and music before and during their diplomacy, 00:08:21 through 00:14:22. Champlain manages to persuade the Algonquin to send a small escort force of their people to accompany Father Laforgue to the Huron mission.

➤ Father Laforgue attempts to explain the concept of heaven and elements of the French language to his escort party and to representatives of another people, the Montagnais. A little person sorcerer, with his face painted bright yellow, declares Laforgue a demon, and the two "priests" encounter each other in a particularly memorable episode, 00:25:32 through 00:38:20.

➤ Influenced by the sorcerer and the other people, the escort party abandons "Black Robe" and Daniel, the other Frenchman, to their fate. Daniel, in love with the chief's daughter, goes after them, and Black Robe prepares to fend for himself. Feeling guilty that they have abandoned him, a few of the party, including the chief and his family, return—only to be captured by a band of Iroquois raiders, 00:48:17 through 00:55:30.

➤ The natives and the Frenchmen are subjected to horrific tortures by the Iroquois, and the chief's young son is killed before his eyes. Black Robe's finger is cut off, and even more violence seems certain to follow, 01:04:18 through 01:09:40.

➤ Laforgue and the others escape, but he goes on alone, still hoping to find the mission to the Hurons. There he discovers only an old, dispirited priest, who, together with his associates, had been blamed for a bout of disease in the region. A group of Hurons tentatively approach Laforgue, asking him, "Do you love us, Black Robe?" When he replies that he does, the leaders agree to be baptized. This culminating scene, between 01:24:02 and 01:37:05, is followed by the simple observation that this group will be massacred by the Iroquois fifteen years later (in 1649).

Discussion Questions

1. Does the film suggest that the native peoples were more brutal than the Europeans?

2. What drives Black Robe? Does he ever have doubts?

3. Is Black Robe so different from the religious officials among the natives?

Further Reading and Viewing

A fascinating collection of documents concerning the *Jesuit Relations* and the images that were made to accompany them and other reports can be found in Allan Greer's *The Jesuit Relations: Natives and Missionaries in Seventeenth-Century North America* (Bedford/St. Martin's, 2000).

Dangerous Liaisons

Film Data

Year: 1988
Director: Stephen Frears
Screenplay: Christopher Hampton, from his play
Production Design: Stuart Craig
Music: George Fenton
Length: 119 minutes
Rating: R

Connection to *The Cultures of the West* by Clifford R. Backman

Chapter 15: "The Enlightened, 1690–1789"

Preview

While there have been several screen adaptations of Pierre-Ambroise-François Choderlos de Laclos's 1782 novel *Les liaisons dangereuses*, this is the only one to incorporate the words of Christopher Hampton's effervescent stage play. The challenge for any adaptation lies in the "epistolary" form of the original novel, ostensibly constructed from a series of letters sent among the main characters and explaining matters from their unique, if oftentimes duplicitous, perspectives. Hampton's script manages to preserve the elements of letter-writing (even when a human backside is used as the writing desk), while summarizing the basic elements of several letter exchanges into brisk, dynamic conversations.

The play, set on the verge of the outbreak of the French Revolution, analyzes the seemingly frivolous lives of a set of aristocrats, as they toy with affections and trample on conventional notions of sexual morality. The film draws into its scope even more of the immediate historical context and the great suffering of the period, showing the utter poverty of Madame de Rosemonde's neighbors and exploring the role of servants in aristocratic households in greater depth. It is not difficult to imagine the post-1789 fate of those who self-righteously boo Madame de Merteuil at the opera or the nuns who tend a heartbroken Madame de Tourvel.

However, the greatest achievements of *Dangerous Liaisons* remain its painstaking attention to period detail, particularly in respect to costume and music, and the skill of its lead actors. Small scenes provide an excerpt from Gluck's *Iphigénie en Tauride* (1779), complete with the staging, costumes, and intimate performance space that were appropriate to the period, and a recital of Händel's instantly recognizable aria *"Ombra mai fù."* While John Malkovich may not have seemed an obvious choice for a professional seducer, his Valmont is appropriately cold and callous—at least before visibly and openly falling in love. Glenn Close's Merteuil is a study in fiercely controlled emotion, and her final outburst of grief and rage at the film's conclusion is truly stunning.

The film is designed to be an intimate analysis of a small circle of people and their overlapping relationships, but there is a profound historical lesson in the original novel. Choderlos de Laclos prefaced his novel—as was standard in the era—with a plea from a fictive "Publisher" and "Editor" of the letters, which they have supposedly "found." This disclaimer of responsibility permitted a degree of distance from the substance of the letters, but Choderlos de Laclos was clearly playing with the convention by locating the novel in the intellectual currents of his own time. The "Publisher" in his *avertissement* ("warning") protests that he cannot believe that these letters, which reveal such wicked morals, could actually date from his own century. After all, in the present century, one "of philosophy," *les lumières* (Enlightened thinkers) "have rendered all the men so honest and all the women so modest and reserved." One could read *Dangerous Liaisons* as a warning against the dangers of excessive reliance on Enlightenment morality. If every moral sensibility is questioned—and ridiculed as old-fashioned or "unenlightened"—how will men and women treat each other?

Recommended Scenes

➢ The film begins with a stirring theme over the grooming rituals of an aristocratic woman (Madame de Merteuil) and a man (the Marquis de Valmont), 00:00:05 through 00:12:22. When they finally meet, it is obvious that they have a long-standing—and intimate—relationship, even though Merteuil, as a supposedly upstanding widow, is obliged to be far more reticent about it in public.

➢ The two rivals in "dangerous liaisons" have set challenges for each other in seduction, and Merteuil attempts to find a suitable candidate to "ruin" her teenaged cousin Cécile de Volanges. In the meantime, Valmont makes a grand display of charity in order to seduce the austere and pious Madame de Tourvel, 00:14:54 through 00:24:14.

➢ In one of the film's most significant scenes, between 00:31:40 and 00:36:42, Merteuil reveals to Valmont how she came to be so opaque to the outside world. Consulting the finest authorities of her day, including philosophers and novelists ("to see what she could get away with"), she has distilled it all to one wonderfully simple principle, "Win or die."

➢ Valmont takes Cécile's virginity—since he and Merteuil both have a grievance against the girl's future husband—and she follows Merteuil's advice to "further her education" under Valmont's tutelage. Merteuil becomes increasingly aware that Valmont's fascination with the lovely Tourvel is more than a professional challenge, 00:48:55 through 01:01:50.

➢ Although Valmont relents at the last minute when seducing Tourvel—who is famous for her morals and love for her absent husband—Merteuil encourages him to press on. He finally achieves "success" in his endeavor, 01:17:01 through 01:24:01.

➢ Merteuil advises Valmont to break off his relationship with Tourvel, since he is becoming a laughingstock among his more cynical friends. When he does, everything unravels, and the two compatriots in seduction become bitter enemies. In a swift series of scenes between 01:35:00 and 01:56:38, Valmont dies in a duel with Cécile's other lover, Tourvel dies of grief, and Merteuil explodes in an agony of self-incrimination and regret. However, the film spares the more hideous fate that awaits her in the novel, where she develops a disease that mars her face, loses all her money, and is forced into exile abroad.

Discussion Questions

1. What explanation does Merteuil give for her behavior?

2. What makes Valmont different?

3. Does the story of *Dangerous Liaisons* demonstrate the dangers of "excessive Enlightenment"?

Further Reading and Viewing

A film tie-in book, featuring Hampton's screenplay, an introduction describing how the play (produced in 1985) eventually became the film (released three years later), and color photographs from the film, was published by Faber and Faber in 1989. Several versions of the original French novel, preserving the epistolary form, are available, and one might particularly be intrigued by the 1958 *Le livre de poche* edition, introduced by the novelist and cultural critic André Malraux.

Jefferson in Paris

Film Data

Year: 1995
Director: James Ivory
Screenplay: Ruth Prawer Jhabvala
Music: Richard Robbins
Length: 139 minutes
Rating: PG-13

Connection to *The Cultures of the West* by Clifford R. Backman

Chapter 16: "The War Against Absolutisms, 1789–1815"

Preview

While *Jefferson in Paris* is one of the less remarkable Merchant-Ivory films, it raises one of the most significant paradoxes in Western, as well as in U.S., history. As Samuel Johnson famously asked in 1775, "How is it that we hear the loudest yelps for liberty among the drivers of Negroes?" Particularly in the 1990s, when DNA evidence confirmed what was long suspected, the hypocrisy of Thomas Jefferson—who declared that "all men are created equal" while fathering children with a woman whose body he owned—seemed an ideal subject for dramatization.

However, this film version adds further layers of complexity and irony by focusing on the period (1785–1789) in which Jefferson was the ambassador of the newly-independent American States to the court of Louis XVI. Resident in Paris just before calls for "Liberty, Equality, Fraternity!" capsized the French monarchy, Jefferson had brought with him his elder daughter Patsy and, eventually, his younger daughter Polly and her enslaved nurse, Sally Hemings. Sally and her brother James were in a unique position in Jefferson's Paris household, because they could, theoretically, have escaped Jefferson's control, as a petition process was available for the slave "property" of foreign nationals. Because it was almost certainly in this period that Jefferson's "relationship" with Sally began, it was also an intriguing question to consider to what extent Sally "consented" to the advances of her master and what promises might have been made on that occasion.

The film also introduces the figure of Maria Cosway, a white—and married—British woman with whom Jefferson must have had an affair in this period, judging from their correspondence. Because he had promised his wife on her deathbed that he would not remarry, Jefferson never sought another woman's hand in marriage, but neither did he deprive himself of female companionship altogether. The film implies that Mrs. Cosway ultimately came to be revolted by the moral horror of Jefferson's slave system and that Jefferson accordingly concentrated his attentions on the vulnerable young woman in his household. Although no more than fifteen years old at the time and thus much younger than her 55-year-old master, Sally produced six children for Jefferson, all of whom he *owned* until they turned twenty-one.

Jefferson in Paris does not shy away from the final, and perhaps the most revealing, irony of all, that Sally Hemings was almost certainly the half-sister of Jefferson's deceased wife. Jefferson's father-in-law had impregnated his slave, and the resulting child was "given," together with other bridal property, to Jefferson when he married Martha Wayles Skelton. Such situations were not at all uncommon among slave-owning aristocrats in the southern States, and yet the film could have been more direct in identifying Jefferson's relationship with Sally Hemings as what it clearly was: coercive rape. Hemings had no choice but to yield to the whims of her master, and her children were used as leverage to keep her under his control. This image is certainly difficult to reconcile with the traditional one concerning "The Sage of Monticello."

Although Jefferson's white descendants were generally opposed to the notion that Jefferson also had African-American descendants, the scientific evidence of the relationship has been declared conclusive. It was perhaps a wise idea to entrust Jefferson's story to an Indian screenwriter whose family had escaped Nazi Germany, and not to an American, who might have been biased in respect to the talismanic effect of Jefferson's name. The result is not perfect, but several ideas of significance are raised in the film, touching on aspects of the revolutionary period and beyond.

Recommended Scenes

➤ Jefferson's slave James Hemings, whom he has brought to Paris, meets with French servants and is told that "People get paid here." Jefferson himself is a bona fide celebrity in the city, and yet he witnesses the gathering storm, as desperately poor people riot for bread in Parisian streets, 00:14:44 through 00:18:37.

➤ Jefferson (played—rather incongruously—by Nick Nolte) is confronted by French intellectuals with the obvious contradiction of a slave owner's having written, "All men are created equal." Jefferson's attractions for Mrs. Cosway grow, and the witticisms of the Versailles court enmesh him further into the delights of Paris, 00:22:26 through 00:29:55.

➤ The Marquis de Lafayette, who had played such a significant role in securing American independence, talks about the revolution with Jefferson. He and other French veterans of this war—who had lost limbs in the service of the independence cause and were promised some amount of financial compensation for their losses—confront Jefferson with the broken promises made by his compatriots in America, 00:36:42 through 00:40:19.

➤ Sally Hemings and her relationship to the deceased Mrs. Jefferson are introduced between 01:06:00 and 01:09:27.

➤ Dr. Guillotin demonstrates a model of his new machine to a group of delighted (if hopelessly naïve) aristocrats, and Jefferson decides to start paying Sally for her work, at least while they are in France, 01:29:24 through 01:36:18. The film strongly implies that Jefferson has already begun having sex with Sally.

➤ In the film's pivotal scene, between 02:03:19 and 02:15:45, Sally reveals to her brother James that she is pregnant, and James confronts the master. James's nagging resentment bubbles to the surface, and Sally miserably realizes her dependence on Jefferson and the Monticello system. To defuse the situation, Jefferson takes a "solemn oath" that he will free Sally's children when they reach legal age and that he will free James soon after they return to Virginia.

Discussion Questions

1. Does the film excuse Jefferson's behavior and attitude in any way?

2. How does the film explore the psychological dimensions of control in a slave system?

3. What might the filmmakers be saying about the contemporary United States, by means of this portrait of a quintessential American?

Further Reading and Viewing

One should view as many Merchant-Ivory films as possible, given their sumptuous look and sophisticated, thoughtful screenplays, but there are also several books that address the themes introduced in *Jefferson in Paris*. Annette Gordon-Reed's *Thomas Jefferson and Sally Hemings: An American Controversy* (University of Virginia Press, 1997) is the strongest and most compelling statement yet of the full consequences of the Hemings revelations, and her conclusions have been reinforced and developed by Henry Wiencek in his polemical *Master of the Mountain: Thomas Jefferson and His Slaves* (Farrar, Straus and Giroux, 2012).

For Jefferson's own disturbing and difficult-to-take pronouncements on race and slavery, see David Waldstreicher's collected volume of *Notes on the State of Virginia, by Thomas Jefferson, with Related Documents* (Bedford/St. Martin's, 2002).

Danton

Film Data

Year: 1983
Director: Andrzej Wajda
Screenplay: Jean-Claude Carrière
Based on the play by Stanisława Przybyzszewska
Music: Jean Prodomides
Length: 136 minutes
Rating: PG

Connection to *The Cultures of the West* by Clifford R. Backman

Chapter 16: "The War Against Absolutisms, 1789–1815"

Preview

The product of a unique collaboration between Western and Eastern Europeans, *Danton* is both a historical investigation of a transformational moment in Western civilization and an artifact of the waning Cold War of the early 1980s. While many saw connections between the French Revolution's spinning out of control in 1794 and the suppression of the Solidarity movement in Poland in 1981 and 1982, Wajda claimed that he had originally found inspiration for the film in a 1932 Polish play on Danton's life and execution. Since the French Revolution was generally viewed in the USSR and Warsaw Pact countries as an inspiration for the Bolshevik Revolution, contemporary statements could be made through comparisons to the major figures of the period. For example, Lenin might be compared to Robespierre, and the means by which they fomented and directed revolution—together with their resort to violence in the name of ideological purity—could be contrasted … albeit cautiously.

When Wajda set about the process of adapting the play to film, he was stymied by the imposition of martial law in Poland in December 1981. Because the generals had forbidden assemblies—and they defined an assembly as any gathering of more than four persons—it appeared impossible to make a film in his country. Undeterred in his ambition to film Danton's story, Wajda contacted a French screenwriter, Jean-Claude Carrière, and sought out funding and suitable actors in France. When he landed Gérard Depardieu for the title role, the money began to flow, and he was allowed to film in the Place de la Concorde (the former Place de la Révolution and the site of the guillotines during the Reign of Terror) and—to his great surprise and relief—in the Assemblée Nationale itself.

Wajda managed to overcome another challenge in the casting of the principal roles in the film. Because he was determined to use a Polish actor, Wojciech Pszoniak, as Robespierre, most of the actors who interacted with him were speaking Polish and their words were dubbed into French. French actors were employed for the scenes involving Danton, and there was only one scene when Pszoniak and Depardieu appeared in the same space, each speaking his own language and with dubbing inserted afterward. Nevertheless, this scene is one of the film's best, and one of Depardieu's improvisations in rehearsal created a memorable encounter.

Many critics around the world saw in Depardieu's ebullient, earthy, and life-loving Danton a reflection of the heroic leader of the Solidarity movement, Lech Wałesa. While Wajda disavowed this connection, it is difficult to avoid, although Wałesa would eventually become president of Poland and not be executed by General Jaruzelski/Robespierre. Danton is a man of appetites, who eats, shouts, and touches actual people, while Robespierre merely orates about popular rights and sovereignty. Wajda believed that the message of *Danton*, promoting human rights and flexibility in reaction to ideological purity, was a significant one in the 1980s and beyond, and he was gratified that the film was re-released in 1989. This year marked not only the bicentennial of the storming of the Bastille, but also the beginning of the end for Communist domination of Eastern Europe.

Recommended Scenes

➢ The film begins with a note that it takes place in Paris in Spring 1794, or "Year II of the Republic." A child in Robespierre's household is prompted to recite from the Declaration of the Rights of Man and of the Citizen, compiled five years earlier for a very different context, 00:02:51 through 00:10:28.

➢ News is received that the Committees of Security and Public Safety have shut down Danton's press mouthpiece and smashed their machines, between 00:26:30 and 00:30:58. Danton remains calm and cheers up his associates, especially Camille and Lucile Desmoulins.

➢ Danton invites Robespierre to his home and confronts him in a blistering encounter, 00:39:24 through 00:48:02. Declaring he would rather be guillotined than a guillotiner, Danton places Robespierre's hands around his neck so he can see what it feels like to actually kill someone.

➢ Danton and his comrades are arrested, but he is still the people's favorite, 01:28:35 through 01:32:15.

➢ Robespierre poses for his portrait in the studio of the artist Jacques-Louis David, 01:40:38 through 01:45:45. Notice particularly the sketches from his painting of the Tennis Court Oath (from which Robespierre suggests that some people be removed, à la Stalin's photographs) and the ongoing work on *The Death of Marat*. Marat had been killed in July 1793 in his bath, and the scene suggests that even more violence is soon to follow.

➢ The culminating moment of the film is reached when the various stages of the guillotining of Danton are depicted, 02:00:02 through 02:13:50. This is one of the few filmed—and realistic—sequences showing the elements of execution by guillotine, and blood drips from the blade as disturbing music plays over the scene. The film ends with the same boy from the film's opening reciting again from the Declaration of the Rights of Man. The words now seem to have a bitter and ironic meaning.

Discussion Questions

1. How does the film deal with the issue of press freedom?

2. Who spoke for "the people" during the Revolution?

3. How does the film warn about the dangers of ideological purity?

Further Reading and Viewing

The Criterion Collection release of *Danton* in 2009 contains a documentary on the making of the film and focuses particularly on responses to it by Poles. A compelling biography of Maximilien Robespierre can be found in Ruth Scurr's aptly titled *Fatal Purity: Robespierre and the French Revolution* (Chatto & Windus, 2006).

Madame Bovary

Film Data

Year: 1991
Director: Claude Chabrol
Based on the novel by Gustave Flaubert
Length: 142 minutes
Rating: PG-13

Connection to *The Cultures of the West* by Clifford R. Backman

Chapter 18: "The Birth of Modern Politics, 1815–1848"

Chapter 21: "The Modern Woman, 1860–1914"

Preview

Gustave Flaubert's 1857 novel *Madame Bovary: Moeurs de province* (*Madame Bovary: Provincial Manners*) is both a landmark in French literature and ripe material for a series of filmmakers. It has been translated into English and adapted for cinema and television in 1932, 1949, 1964, 1975, and 2000, but Claude Chabrol's film—and Isabelle Huppert's brittle, energetic performance—capture the spirit of the novel in its best light. Chabrol was a prominent director in the French "New Wave" school best known for thrillers like *Les biches* (1968) and *Le boucher* (*The Butcher*, 1970). Chabrol specialized in directing female actors in particular, and Huppert's sudden outbursts and impulsive movements perfectly replicate the spirit of a frustrated, trapped, but ever romantic Emma Bovary.

Flaubert set his novel in Yonville, near Rouen in Normandy, and the subtitle suggests the essentially "provincial" application of his story. Furthermore, he placed the Bovarys' struggles in the period of the "Citizen King" Louis Philippe (1830–1848), with a dispiriting agricultural fair as one of the novel's more excruciatingly "provincial" moments. The novel focuses on the frustrations of a woman who is seeking more romance and excitement than her dull husband can give, and she launches herself into ill-advised affairs and excessive expenditures, finally killing herself to escape the crushing debts she has contracted with the sinister M. Lheureux. The film, like the novel, stresses the unique situation of a woman who is condemned to a life of domesticity, sewing, supervising household chores, and listening to her husband drone on about his day at the office. Emma dreams of a life beyond Yonville and finds the charms of the handsome Rodolphe Boulanger irresistible. When she falls again for the young Léon, she is swept off her feet by his declaration, concerning making love in a carriage, "*Cela se fait à Paris!*" "They do it in Paris!" Emma is trapped in provincial reality, when she longs to escape to cosmopolitan romance. Chabrol's film explains both the appeal of Romanticism and its capacity to crush the spirit, and the story of *Madame Bovary* marks a significant point of transition in the arts.

Recommended Scenes

➢ Charles Bovary pays visits on Emma, the daughter of one of his patients, and her whimsical nature flashes out even at this early stage, 00:06:32 through 00:12:37. She allows herself to be married, but it is clear that she is still unhappy and longing to escape to the city.

➢ Soon bored with her husband, Emma is captivated by the opportunity to waltz at a ball and she experiences "the best evening of her life," 00:15:31 through 00:22:29.

➢ M. Lheureux, the draper and moneylender, recognizes Emma's romantic longings and offers to supply her needs … all she need do is sign a promissory note, 00:38:35 through 00:41:26.

➢ Rodolphe also recognizes Emma's longings and her desperation for romance. He makes short work of seducing her, 00:53:08 through 01:02:22.

➢ Because of Emma's prompting, Charles botches a surgery to repair the club foot of Hippolyte, a young disabled man in Yonville. Charles's failure to secure fame in his profession earns even more contempt from his wife, 01:19:05 through 01:26:02.

➢ After Rodolphe has cast her off, Emma falls in love, again, with a younger man who has returned to Yonville after some time in Paris, between 01:38:37 and 01:43:31.

➢ Still unhappy and unlucky in love, Emma contracts even more debts, and M. Lheureux insists that she begin paying the money back, 01:54:12 through 02:01:26.

➢ When Rodolphe refuses to help, Emma takes arsenic from the shop of M. Homais, the local pharmacist, and dies in agony, 02:06:16 through 02:19:46.

Discussion Questions

1. Is the film primarily concerned with Emma's frustration, as a woman in a male-dominated society?

2. How does *Madame Bovary* develop the contrast between rural and urban life?

3. What does the story suggest about the dangers of Romantic novels and attitudes?

Further Reading and Viewing

The novel can still be read, in a variety of excellent and up-to-date translations, and one might also examine a fan site, http://www.madamebovary.com/, described by its authors as "a labor of love" for the novel.

Angels & Insects

Film Data

Year: 1995
Director: Philip Haas
Screenplay by Philip Haas and Belinda Haas
Based on the novella *Morpho Eugenia*, by A. S. Byatt
Costume Designer: Paul Brown
Music: Alexander Balanescu
Length: 118 minutes
Rating: R

Connection to *The Cultures of the West* by Clifford R. Backman

Chapter 20: "The God Problem, 1799–1907"

Preview

Best known for her novel *Possession* (1990), which followed scholars of Victorian literature in their investigation of a long-buried relationship, A. S. Byatt returned to the mid-Victorian period in her short but ambitious novella *Morpho Eugenia* (1992). Byatt's fiction often hinges on the intellectual excitement of delving into the past, and this novel tackles a very large subject, i.e. the earth-shattering challenges posed, particularly to religious and ethical thought, by the scientific advances of Charles Darwin. Rather than detailing Darwin's life, or those of any actual people in the Britain of his era, Byatt constructs a story set on a fictional estate in the early 1860s, just after the publication of Darwin's *On the Origin of Species* (1859).

Her central character, William Adamson (the names in the novel are all evocative) hails from a part of Yorkshire that "consisted of foul black places amongst fields and rough land of great beauty," and, in his boyhood, was drawn to collecting samples of plants and insects in those fields and then studying them. Emerging from this cocoon as a professional naturalist, Adamson was transplanted to the Amazon basin, where he collected more samples and made further investigations of a habitat teeming with life. Returning to England, he was shipwrecked and spent fifteen harrowing days on a lifeboat in the Atlantic. As the novella opens, in 1860, he has been invited to stay at the home of Harald Alabaster, charged with organizing and classifying an impressive collection of plant and animal samples Alabaster has acquired over several years.

Over the course of the novel, Adamson is brought into the circle of Alabaster's family, forms a close working relationship with the younger children's governess, Matilda (Matty) Crompton, composes a book about the insect life on the Alabaster estate entitled *The Swarming City* … and makes a shocking and horrible discovery toward the end of the story. *Morpho Eugenia* is thus a traditional piece of fiction, though one that engages, in a profound and thoughtful way, with the intellectual tidal wave that came crashing upon sedate Victorians in the form of "evolution by means of natural selection." The highlights of the novel involve Adamson's conversations with Lord Alabaster, who has taken holy orders in the Church of England and is deeply troubled about the full implications of Darwin's theory, which seems to him to call into doubt God's existence. Adamson speaks with confidence about the rationality and scientific acumen of Darwin's investigations, but his confidence in scientific progress is badly shaken when he discovers a strange and "unnatural" relationship in his own household.

The filmed version of this rich and complex story is particularly remarkable for its use of color and a complex visual palette. The costumes of the women, in particular, are deliberately designed to mirror the insects that Adamson and his associates are studying. By these means, the so-called "angels" of the mid-Victorian home can literally be viewed as "insects," following their instincts in maintaining the needs of themselves and their "hive." In her drab, austere clothes that are so different from the brilliant gowns of Eugenia Alabaster, Kristin Scott Thomas, as Matty Crompton, manages to stay invisible to Adamson until the final scenes. The two scientists escape Bredely Hall to further researches in South America, and perhaps they will eventually find themselves on Darwin's famous Galapagos Islands…?

Recommended Scenes

➢ The opening credits profile the exuberant dances and mating rituals Adamson had encountered in the Amazon, and the scene dissolves to its European equivalent, a ball in progress on an English estate, 00:00:05 through 00:07:20.

➢ In a dinnertime conversation, Adamson and Lord Alabaster (joined by Miss Crompton) discuss Mr. Darwin's theories about why the male of the species is often so much more adorned and elaborate in his coloring than the female, 00:11:30 through 00:16:39.

Eugenia, the most beautiful and eligible of Alabaster's many daughters, later appears in a fantastic bee-like costume, and she asks Adamson about life among the "savages."

➤ Adamson takes Miss Crompton and her young charges on nature "rambles" on the estate, and he leaps high in the social order by convincing Eugenia to marry him. Nevertheless, as he is often reminded by his frequently drunk and invariably belligerent brother-in-law Edgar, he is "not one of us," and it becomes clear that his sole purpose is to squire more squires on Eugenia.

➤ In the meantime, Adamson throws himself into his close observations of insect life on the grounds of the Hall, discovering Matty's drawing ability and discovering in her the intellectual stimulation that he lacks in his wife, 00:51:53 through 00:56:50.

➤ In the crucial scenes of the film, 01:11:20 through 01:21:22, William and Matty discover a "slaving raid" by one group of ants against another, and they, naturally, discuss the ongoing Civil War in the United States. (One is reminded of Thoreau's "Battle of the Ants" in *Walden* [1854].) Their anthropomorphic descriptions of the raid's progress are followed by a rich and wide-ranging discussion between Adamson and Harald about God and nature post-Darwin.

➤ William discovers a shocking secret that everyone else in the household, including Matty, apparently already knows, and a new, more intimate relationship springs up between William and Matty, 01:37:31 through 01:50:50.

Discussion Questions

1. How does the film compare the mores of "civilized" people in England with those of the "savages" elsewhere?

2. How and why does the film compare human and insect life?

3. How does Darwinian theory undermine Lord Alabaster's faith in God?

Further Reading and Viewing

A superb communal biography of the many prominent individuals who began to question and lose their Christian faith in the nineteenth century can be found in A. N. Wilson's *God's Funeral: The Decline of Faith in Western Civilization* (W.W. Norton, 1999). The title of the book is borrowed from a poem by Thomas Hardy, in which God is literally carried to his grave by mourners who wonder what, if anything, will replace their deity. The impact of Darwinian thought, in particular, recurs throughout this book.

Zulu

Film Data

Year: 1964
Director: Cy Endfield
Screenplay: John Prebble and Cy Endfield
Music: John Bury
Length: 138 minutes
Rating: No rating

Connection to *The Cultures of the West* by Clifford R. Backman

Chapter 22: "The Great Land Grab, 1880–1914"

Preview

Zulu is both a celebration of the "heroism" of a small contingent of British troops who held off a Zulu army in January 1879 and a product of the era of European withdrawal from their colonial holdings. The story was inspired by a battle at Rorke's Drift in South Africa, just after a disastrous defeat for the British at Isandlwana, and it provides extensive portraits of the English and Welsh soldiers in this small frontier unit. Very little attention is given in the film to the Zulu warriors who were defending their homeland against European invasion, although the historical Chief Cetewayo of the Zulu makes a brief appearance early in the film.

It is critical to bear in mind the immediate context of this film. For one example, Kenya had been granted its independence by the British government in 1963, after the Mau Mau Uprising had captured British attention throughout the 1950s—and, only in July 2012, the U.K. government admitted to having used torture and sexual abuse against rebels in the period. South Africa had imposed its draconian apartheid regime of racial segregation and subjugation of the majority black population in 1948, and pressure would mount throughout the 1960s and 1970s for the British government and the British Commonwealth to take a stand against these and similar abuses in Rhodesia (today's Zimbabwe). It may seem counterintuitive to have made a movie about British soldiers at the early stages of the "New Imperialism" within this significant moment of retrenchment from colonial hegemony.

However, there may be a subtext in *Zulu*, offering respect and appreciation for the skills of the determined warriors who resisted colonial incursions … at least in the nineteenth century.

The film opens on the catastrophic (for the British) defeat at Isandlwana, one of the few instances in which colonial powers were turned back, if temporarily, by native troops. *Zulu* was made, as its end credits attest, with the cooperation of the current Zulu Chief Buthelezi, and it was filmed in Natal, employing Zulu extras. As per South Africa's apartheid laws, the extras could not be paid, but the filmmakers left behind animals and the implements from their sets, which may have been some compensation. The Boer War is also prefigured in the screenplay, with the appearance of a Boer farmer who advises the British— and who demonstrates the skillful and advanced tactics that had been developed by the Zulu army. The film presents the Zulu as merely the enemy, but the soldiers and other personnel at the fort often ask why this war is necessary. None of the questions receives a satisfactory answer, and that may have been the director's intention.

Recommended Scenes

➢ The disaster at Isandlwana, in which roughly 1,500 British troops (and very likely many more Zulu) had been killed, is mentioned, and the scene opens on an exuberant Zulu celebration attended by a Swedish missionary and his daughter. The customs of Europeans and Africans are compared, and Cetewayo makes a comment to the Reverend Witt, 00:01:35 through 00:13:02.

➢ Michael Caine, playing the upper-class and rather irritating commander Bromhead, is introduced, and it is clear that he will come to loggerheads with the fort's engineer Chard, 00:25:33 through 00:30:31.

➢ News arrives of the defeat at Isandlwana, together with further news of a coming attack by four thousand Zulu warriors on the fort, which can only muster one hundred British defenders. Reverend Witt delivers a pacifist message, and forty native troops abandon the fort, 00:51:25 through 00:56:46.

➢ Zulu warriors appear on the ridge, and they beat their shields in sight of the fort, shouting their battle cry "Usuthu!" to terrify the defenders. This is an effective tactic, but the defenders fire volleys of guns at the first waves of Zulu attackers. The remainder continues chanting and massing for further attack, 01:05:55 through 01:13:10.

➤ Sniper units among the Zulu are shown, and the film moves repeatedly from the Zulu faces to British ones. A grievously wounded soldier asks the simple question, "Why?," between 01:20:47 and 01:30:54.

➤ The culminating moment of the film displays a contingent of Welshmen (of course, given the Welsh reputation for choral singing) in full-throated hymn singing, designed to answer a song by the Zulu, 01:58:33 through 02:06:08. The British fire in ranks on the Zulu, and yet the native troops keep pressing on. The engagement ends with piles of Zulu corpses around the successfully defended fort.

➤ The few survivors are relieved, but they receive word that another massive group of Zulu are heading toward the fort. However, this group of Zulu begins singing because they are, they are told, "saluting fellow braves" on the British side. The film ends by noting the Victoria Crosses that were given to the real men profiled throughout, 02:10:41 through 02:18:30.

Discussion Questions

1. Does the film glorify British militarism, at least in the nineteenth century?

2. What role does Adendorff the Boer play in the film?

3. Is Reverend Witt's pacifist message taken seriously?

Further Reading and Viewing

A segment of the video series "History's Turning Points," produced in 1995, profiles the Battle of Isandlwana, focusing in particular on the goals of Cetewayo and of Theophilus Shepstone, who presided over the annexation of the Transvaal in 1877 and ruled South Africa from Pretoria in this period.

Wilde

Film Data

Year: 1997
Director: Brian Gilbert
Screenplay: Julian Mitchell
Based on the biography *Oscar Wilde*, by Richard Ellmann
Length: 117 minutes
Rating: R

Connection to *The Cultures of the West* by Clifford R. Backman

Chapter 23: "From Nihilism to Modernism, 1880–1939"

Preview

Wilde was released one hundred years after Oscar Wilde was released from prison, after a two-year sentence with hard labor for the crime of "gross indecency." Having suffered a severe blow to his health in prison and living under the shame and humiliation of his treatment in the court and in the court of public opinion, Wilde died in Paris in 1900 at the age of forty-six. He left behind a legacy of brilliant plays, short stories, children's tales, and a novel—all of which are profiled, to some extent, in the ambitious screenplay of this film. Moreover, the way he chose to live his life and to express himself and his passions represent the shifting attitudes of fin-de-siècle culture in the West. Although he was made to suffer, his attitudes, opinions, and aphorisms continue to shock and delight, and his career represents a crucial step in the necessary liberation of those who experience "the love that dare not speak its name," even in our own time.

The film's screenplay explores one of the fundamental questions posed to biographers of Wilde: why did he choose to begin a relationship with Lord Alfred Douglas ("Bosie"), a man who seemed so far beneath him in temperament and talent? The film suggests what anyone who has been in love knows, that love is oftentimes difficult to explain, and one's passions often seem irrational to those who are standing outside the situation. Determined to cover a wide segment of Wilde's artistic, as well as his personal, achievements, Julian Mitchell inserted references to *The Picture of Dorian Gray* (Oscar actually has an affair, in the film, with a handsome young man named Mr. Gray), his plays *An Ideal Husband, Lady Windermere's Fan, The Importance of Being Earnest,* and *Salome,* and, after his trial, "The Ballad of Reading Gaol" and "De Profundis." He even describes the gestation of the story "The Selfish Giant," through snippets of the story told to his two sons at various moments in the film, and parallels between Wilde's life and that of his "Giant" are nicely brought out by these means.

However, the best parts of the film are probably those that focus on Wilde's relationship with his wife, Constance Lloyd Wilde. The screenplay emphasizes her suffering in the midst of her husband's public humiliation, and in his frequent neglect of her and her children. She may not have been aware of her husband's proclivities and homosexual liaisons, but the screenplay is unflinching in demonstrating her pain and Oscar's guilt at having caused it. Stephen Fry was, of course, an inspired choice to play Oscar, resembling him physically and making Wilde's actual witticisms (and those that were brilliantly invented by the screenwriter to sound Wildean) seem as fresh and clever as when they were first delivered.

Recommended Scenes

➢ The film demonstrates Oscar's domestic happiness with Constance, but there remains the undercurrent of his attraction to the "rent boys" whom he encounters on the street. His friend Robbie Ross introduces him to the pleasures he has always longed to experience, 00:08:35 through 00:15:08.

➢ Oscar meets, and is instantly charmed by, Bosie Douglas between 00:24:52 and 00:33:45. Bosie's strained relationship with his bullying father, the marquess of Queensberry, is mentioned, and the physical side of the relationship is explored.

➢ Strains in the relationship begin to appear, and Bosie frequently lashes out at Oscar for being "middle-class" in attitude and behavior. Wilde's makes a favorable impression on Bosie's father, but the homophobic remarks of the marquess suggest that future difficulties lie in wait, 00:42:46 through 00:55:59.

➢ Bosie's father accuses Wilde of "posing as a somdomite [the misspelling is preserved in the film]," and Wilde decides to prosecute for libel—over the (sensible, as it turned out) objections of Robbie, 01:11:00 through 01:20:29.

➢ When Wilde loses his case and the Crown threatens to prosecute him for "gross indecency" (based on revelations made during the first trial), Wilde again refuses to take the safer course and decides to stay in England. His trial proceeds, and he is condemned to prison, 01:25:50 through 01:36:54.

➢ Out of prison, Wilde still wishes to see Bosie, and the captions note that he died soon after. The end titles incorporate images of the illustrations from his books, 01:48:44 through 01:56:43.

Discussion Questions

1. Does the film make a compelling argument for the validity of "the love that dare not speak its name"?

2. Does the film explain why Wilde chose to love Bosie?

3. How did Wilde reflect fin-de-siècle sensibilities?

Further Reading and Viewing

The one hundredth anniversaries of Wilde's trial and death sparked renewed interest in this important cultural figure, and the ongoing struggle for GLBT rights in the United States and throughout the world makes him a historical figure that always repays reexamination. An even better treatment of Wilde's final years can be found in David Hare's 1998 play, *The Judas Kiss*, and a new examination of his wife is available in Franny Moyle's *Constance: The tragic and scandalous life of Mrs. Oscar Wilde* (John Murray Press, 2012).

Passchendaele

Film Data

Year: 2008
Director: Paul Gross
Screenplay: Paul Gross
Music: Jan A. P. Kaczmarek
Length: 115 minutes
Rating: R

Connection to *The Cultures of the West* by Clifford R. Backman

Chapter 24: "The World at War (Part I), 1914–1920"

Preview

This profile of a Canadian soldier in World War I was written and directed by the actor best known (in the United States) for his performance as a Mountie in the 1990s television series *Due South*. Inspired by his grandfather's description of having killed a young German soldier by stabbing him through the forehead, Gross developed the story of a man whose memories of a similar experience haunt him and make him question the correctness of the "patriotic" cause for which he is fighting. The film is thus a meditation on the meaning of this "War to End All Wars," as well as an important supplement to the existing body of films and books about World War I, which generally ignore the contributions of the "Dominions" to the Allied war cause. The opening captions remind audiences that, even though Canada was a small country of eight million people, 600,000 men were sent to the Western Front between 1914 and 1918. A tenth of those men never came home.

The film unapologetically details the sufferings of soldiers at the front, and it also points to the anxieties and violence that could plague the home front as well. Calgary, Alberta, a young city on the Canadian frontier, is the main setting of the film, and the hero, Sergeant Michael Dunne, comes to lose faith in the righteousness of the British Empire in this European war. Sent home wounded and shell-shocked (he sardonically refers to his official diagnosis as "battle fatigue"), he falls in love with his nurse, who is treating her own less visible wounds with a drug addiction. A mob descends on Sarah's house, vandalizing it because her father had returned to his native Germany at the beginning of the war and had died fighting on the German side. Michael returns to the front, not for any devotion to the Imperial cause, but only in order to watch over Sarah's brother, who has enlisted to erase the shame of his family.

Passchendaele provides no easy answers, and it asks particularly relevant questions about the necessity of wars and the true reasons why men and women fight them. Michael's experience in a recruiting office reinforces his disdain for patriotic appeals, and his odious British supervisor barely hides his contempt for the "colonials" the British require to fill out their ranks. The film's central image is that of a handsome adolescent, who could be a Canadian as easily as a German, reaching out his hand to a soldier and asking "*Kamerad?*"—only to have a bayonet blade stabbed between his eyes.

Recommended Scenes

➤ The film opens with scenes from a battlefield in France or Belgium in 1915, with German machine gunners in a bombed-out church besieged by four Canadian soldiers. Their commander, Michael Dunne, throws a grenade into the church, stabs the surviving German with his bayonet, and is then wounded in an explosion, 00:04:22 through 00:07:18.

➤ Returned home to Calgary, Dunne reveals that his three brothers have been killed in the war—and that his mother has died of a broken heart, hearing that he too was wounded. In his new job for the "war effort," at a recruiting station, he is told to be on the lookout for "saboteurs" and "provocateurs" in Calgary, 00:15:09 through 00:25:06.

➤ The natural beauty of Alberta is revealed as Michael rides horses with Sarah Mann, between 00:31:57 and 00:36:55.

➤ Sarah's home is vandalized, and Michael learns the reason from his bigoted commander at the recruiting station, 00:41:53 through 00:46:03.

➤ Michael follows Sarah's brother back to the war and is given a new place in command by a sympathetic Canadian officer near Passchendaele, Belgium, 01:08:28 through 01:17:01. The resulting conflict, for control of a critical section of Belgium, took place in the fall of 1917 and is also known as the Third Battle of Ypres.

➤ Slogging through lashing rain, thick mud, and volleys of machine-gun fire, Michael and the other Canadians labor to make incremental progress. Michael finds Sarah's brother David crucified with barbed wire and planks in No Man's Land. Michael "takes up the cross" and carries David back to the Canadian lines, although he dies in the effort, 01:25:47 through 01:41:04.

➤ Sarah, David (in a wheelchair), and others gather at Michael's grave in Alberta, and the camera pans to all the other crosses in the field. The end credits incorporate film footage from the war itself, 01:45:45 through 01:52:20.

Discussion Questions

1. How does the film describe the dangers of excessive patriotism?

2. How does the film develop the idea of Canadian nationalism and distinctiveness from the U.K.?

3. Could *Passchendaele* be considered an anti-war statement?

Further Reading and Viewing

Stanley Kubrick's 1957 film *Paths of Glory* covers some of the same territory as *Passchendaele*, although it profiles a group of French soldiers who were shot in exemplary punishment for "cowardice."

Triumph des Willens (Triumph of the Will)

Film Data

Year: 1935
Director: Leni Riefenstahl
Length: 110 minutes
Rating: No rating

Connection to *The Cultures of the West* by Clifford R. Backman

Chapter 25: "Radical Realignments, 1919–1939"

Preview

The official film of the Nazi Party's Nuremberg rally, held between September 4 and 10 1934, *Triumph of the Will* is surely the most controversial film ever made, and it is the only one in this book that is itself a historical artifact. It is also unique in that is the only film here to have been directed and supervised by a woman. Because of this film and its propaganda effect, Riefenstahl was effectively shut out of the filmmaking world after 1945. Accused of being a collaborator with the Nazi regime, she was detained at various points in Allied custody and confronted with charges. However, she was ultimately released, proclaiming—as she would for the next six decades—that she was not personally responsible for the violence perpetrated by Nazi Germany.

Turning her artistic attentions to photography, Riefenstahl went on to document the lives of the Nuba people in the Sudan and would, in her 70s, 80s, and 90s, take her camera underwater, capturing wonderful images of marine wildlife and coral reefs. Whatever her subject matter, however, her work was condemned for its "fascist aesthetic" which had been, according to her many critics, inculcated in the 1930s and carefully nurtured ever afterward. When she was interviewed for a 1993 documentary on her "*Wonderful, Horrible Life,*" Riefenstahl protested that she had produced an "artistic film" and not a "political film" in *Triumph of the Will*. If the Nazi Party conference had been composed of "vegetables or fruit" instead of speeches, she would have been driven by the same overriding concern: to make the film as "interesting" as possible.

Stage-managed by Albert Speer, the Nuremberg rally was captured by means of a series of innovative camera angles, and Riefenstahl even had her camera crew wear roller skates and install moving cameras on flagpoles in order to achieve dynamic shots at critical moments. Castigated for enhancing Hitler's image in the speeches that highlight the film, she, again in the 1993 documentary, averred that when an artist is filming a speech, whether its subject is "trees, fish, or politics," it has to be trimmed to make it "interesting." Two-hour speeches had to be condensed to five minutes, and she claimed not to have cared about—or even much listened to—what Hitler was actually saying. The film constantly shifts from Hitler to the crowd and back again, stressing the solitary individual and his sway over exuberant, cheering masses.

Riefenstahl's artistic genius is generally acknowledged and her expert handling of many technical challenges resulted in international acclaim in Europe and North America in the late 1930s. She was particularly renowned for her ability to connect movement to music, and she observed that the editing process alone required five months' work, virtually around the clock. She remains, even after her death in 2003 at the age of 101, an extremely complex historical figure, and her artistic legacy continues to be reinterpreted and reassessed. Her achievement in the medium of film poses the question of the artist's moral responsibility for the effects of his/her creation, and whether the simple claim of "not being political" is sufficient.

Recommended Scenes

➤ A series of opening captions announces the date of the rally as being, for one example, nineteen months after the beginning of the German *Wiedergeburt* ("Regeneration"). The captions dissolve into the mist, and Hitler's airplane descends through this mist over Nuremberg, 00:02:19 through 00:06:20.

➤ A night rally is held at Hitler's hotel, complete with torches, electric light bulbs, and floodlights, 00:11:09 through 00:14:02. The images are designed to recall the night of January 30, 1933, when Hitler was greeted as the new Reichskanzler with a torchlit parade, prompting an observer to note that the Nazi government was *der Sprung ins Dunkle*, "a leap in the dark."

➤ One of the most frequently referenced elements of the film is the mass demonstration of the Reich Labor Service, between 00:34:17 and 00:41:18. The men in the unit hold and present their shovels exactly like rifles, and a worshipful young man calls upon each of his *Kameraden* to name their hometowns. The final one notes that he is from "the Saar," which was of particular relevance in 1934.

➤ Hitler speaks before a rally of the Hitler Youth (*Hitler Jugend* or HJ), between 00:47:44 and 00:55:10. The camera moves along beside his platform and gazes up at him, as the audience is enjoined to do as well.

➤ Hitler, Himmler, and the new (after the violent removal of Ernst Röhm a few months earlier) and more malleable SA (*Sturmabteilung*) commander lay a wreath at a memorial to President Hindenburg, 01:05:07 through 01:16:43. The image of three figures strolling past assembled masses has been copied many times, from *Return of the Jedi* to *Gladiator*, and one of the moving cameras, attached to a flagpole, can be seen on its upward trajectory in the shot.

➤ Hitler offers his final speech of the rally, reminding the audience that the NSDAP (the Nazi Party) was once composed of only seven members and now it is composed of millions, 01:40:05 through 01:48:15. Hitler's distinctive style of speech, involving upward gazes, emphatic hand gestures, and accelerating passion, is captured effectively in this scene, and many of these elements would assist Charles Chaplin in his masterful parody of Hitler, as "Adenoid Hynkel" in *The Great Dictator* (1940).

Discussion Questions

1. Does the film convey historical information, specifically about the inner workings of Hitler's government?

2. Is there a detectable theme in *Triumph of the Will*?

3. How are young people and youth culture incorporated into the film?

Further Reading and Viewing

It is particularly valuable to watch the three-hour 1993 German documentary on the director's life and career, released under its English title *The Wonderful, Horrible Life of Leni Riefenstahl.* The segment of the film dealing with *Triumph of the Will* is especially fascinating, since the interviewer is himself making a documentary and Riefenstahl is explaining her challenges and solutions to a fellow artist. However, it is eerie to watch the look of fascination steal over Riefenstahl's ninety-year-old face as she exults in her artistic statement from many years earlier.

Im toten Winkel: Hitlers Sekretärin
(*Blind Spot: Hitler's Secretary*)

Film Data

Year: 2002
Director: André Heller
Camera and Sound: Othmar Schmiderer
Editor: Daniel Pöhacker
Length: 87 minutes
Rating: PG

Connection to *The Cultures of the West* by Clifford R. Backman

Chapter 26: "The World at War (Part II), 1937–1945"

Preview

Like *Triumph of the Will*, *Blind Spot* is essentially a documentary that conveys a vision of the Third Reich, principally through the eyes of a woman who was closely connected to that regime. In both cases, "blindness" is an apt metaphor, though Traudl Junge, shortly before the end of her life, seems to have had glimpses of her true role in and responsibility for the depredations of Nazism. Born in Bavaria in 1920, Junge became Adolf Hitler's private secretary in late 1942, and she remained in his service until the very end of his life in April 1945. Her memories of the critical weeks in the bunker in Berlin in April and May 1945 are among the most fascinating and disturbing records of the Nazi era, and they, together with the memoirs of Albert Speer and other sources, formed the basis for the 2004 film *Der Untergang* (*Downfall*).

This film is an edited version of a series of interviews conducted with Junge in 2001, a few months before her death. The camera rarely moves as Junge describes the oftentimes banal details of her working relationship with Hitler. However, the result is a chilling revelation of the complex internal life of a rather ordinary elderly woman. The most innovative aspect of the film is its focus on Junge while she watches previously-taped footage of herself and reacts to the interviewer about her own seemingly incorrect and incomplete statements. The film captures her coming to terms, at least partially, with her own past and her naïveté at this early point in her life.

Having emerged from the bunker and having been briefly imprisoned by the Soviet and American armies, Junge was freed under terms of *die Jugendamnestie*, an amnesty designed specifically for "young fellow travelers" or "misguided youth" who were caught up in Nazism but were believed to pose no real threat to society since Hitler had been eliminated. By the end of the film, Junge comes to see that "it is no excuse to be young," especially when she compares herself to the resistor Sophie Scholl, who was close to her own age. *Blind Spot* is thus a mesmerizing study in conscience and the necessity to rethink and reexamine what we have done and witnessed throughout our lives.

Recommended Scenes

➤ The themes of "blindness" and "seeing oneself" in a true light are reinforced when Junge views previously filmed footage of herself, between 00:03:12 and 00:06:22. She admits that she liked Hitler, and this makes her question whether she simply didn't notice or chose not to pay attention to the evil he represented.

➤ Junge explains how she came to find herself in Hitler's employ, tracing her thwarted ambition to be a dancer and then her falling into office work. Having become a finalist for the position of Hitler's private secretary, she met him in an interview and found him a "*gemütlich* (kindly, warm, sympathetic) older gentleman," 00:10:30 through 00:17:39. She does not admit here, though *Der Untergang* strongly suggests this to be the case, that it was her Bavarian background that actually won her the job.

➤ A compelling section of the film concerns Hitler's relationship with his beautiful and clever dog Blondi, 00:25:23 through 00:31:10. Hitler's German shepherd is well known from many sources, but, having retailed some anecdotes about her, Junge admits that much of what she's saying may seem banal. Nevertheless, she thinks it is important to stress Hitler's human qualities and interests.

➤ Junge provides a fascinating narrative of Hitler's marriage to Eva Braun in the bunker, while Russian bombs were exploding everywhere overhead. A significant section of her interview concerns her typing of Hitler's last will and testament, 01:08:12 through 01:15:00.

➢ Junge describes the horror of the deaths, by cyanide, of the Goebbelses' six children, and she claims that she heard the gunshot that marked Hitler's suicide, even though she was not sure what the sound was at the time, 01:17:07 through 01:21:56.

➢ After the captions reveal her amnesty and her later career, Junge observes that she had always thought that she was misguided and naïve because she was young. But her attitude changed when she saw a memorial to Sophie Scholl, whose "White Rose" resistance organization was violently suppressed by the regime in 1943.

Discussion Questions

1. Is Junge's statement that Hitler "never mentioned Jews specifically" at all credible?

2. What do Junge's references to dogs and children indicate about her, and about Hitler?

3. Is it "no excuse to be young," as Junge wearily admits?

Further Reading and Viewing

Downfall raised much controversy in Germany and elsewhere, as there was a fear that the focus on Hitler's final days in the bunker might elicit sympathy for him and for Nazism generally. However, the film should be viewed, if only for the masterful performances of Bruno Ganz (as Hitler) and of Alexandra Maria Lara as Traudl Junge.

Dr. Strangelove or: How I Learned to Stop Worrying and Love the Bomb

Film Data

Year: 1964
Director: Stanley Kubrick
Screenplay: Stanley Kubrick, Peter George, and Terry Southern
Suggested by the novel *Red Alert*, by Peter George
Length: 95 minutes
Rating: PG

Connection to *The Cultures of the West* by Clifford R. Backman

Chapter 27: "A Theater of the Absurd, 1945–1968"

Preview

Dr. Strangelove provides ample proof of the capacity of humor, and especially very black humor, to combat institutionalized madness. "Mutually Assured Destruction" was the order of the day, especially in the wake of the Cuban Missile Crisis of October 1962. In a speech to the United Nations General Assembly in September 1961, President Kennedy had described the nuclear arsenals of the United States and the Soviet Union as "a sword of Damocles" hanging over our collective heads. In his estimation, "Every man, woman and child lives under a nuclear sword of Damocles, hanging by the slenderest of threads, capable of being cut at any moment by accident, or miscalculation, or by madness. The weapons of war must be abolished before they abolish us."

This "slenderest of threads" was very nearly severed a year later, and the reality of nuclear weaponry—and the possibility that a rogue agent could accumulate and detonate nuclear material—hangs over our heads, even today. The original intention of the masterful director Stanley Kubrick (1928–1999) was to adapt Peter George's completely serious and high-minded thriller *Red Alert* directly to the screen. An early, and initially dismissed, idea of transforming it into a comedy eventually returned to his mind, and the result was surely the funniest but also one of the most disturbing films ever made. In this scenario, a rogue general, Jack D. Ripper, seizes control of Burpleson Air Force Base and launches a flotilla of planes to drop nuclear bomb on their targets in the Soviet Union. Because he believes that "war is too important to be left to politicians," General Ripper is launching a pre-emptive strike to combat a Communist plot "to sap and impurify all of our precious bodily fluids." All but one of the planes are recalled, but the Soviet Ambassador reveals that a "Doomsday device" has been installed beneath all Russian facilities that will detonate automatically once a bomb is dropped. While the U.S. Air Force issued a disclaimer that an accident of this sort could never happen, Kubrick's film does not really cause us to end our "worry" and make us "love the bomb." The film does, however, make us laugh in "shock and awe" at the brilliant lines of Kubrick and Southern's screenplay and at the masterful performance of Peter Sellers, cast in three roles and speaking BBC British, Middle American, and, best of all, excitable German. From the obviously sexual imagery of the opening airplane refueling sequence to the exploding mushroom clouds over the final "We'll Meet Again" number, Kubrick employed all the best elements of filmmaking into a devastating portrait of a world gone unutterably and irretrievably mad.

Recommended Scenes

➢ Plan R is initiated, by Jack D. Ripper's orders, and President Muffley seeks advice from his military and civilian advisors in the war room, 00:19:40 through 00:31:25. While he is not condoning Ripper's behavior, General Buck Turgidson (George C. Scott, chomping gum and speaking with his mistress on the phone at intervals) says that it's too early to judge and condemn him for "a single slip-up."

➢ In some of the film's most hilarious sequences, President Muffley (Sellers) tries to calm down the Soviet Premier Kissoff on the telephone, and Ripper explains his theory about fluoridation and the impurity of "fluids," 00:37:35 through 00:57:25.

➢ Major "King" Kong rides the bomb into Laputa (a name borrowed from Jonathan Swift), inside the Soviet Union, in one of cinema's iconic moments. Dr. Strangelove (Sellers again) sketches out his plans for surviving nuclear cataclysm, and mushroom clouds explode to the strains of Vera Lynn's cheery song, 01:24:54 through 01:34:41.

Discussion Questions

1. Is the film merely an exercise in black comedy?

2. Could the film be interpreted as anti-American or as overly contemptuous of American leadership during the Cold War?

3. How does the film reflect its specific place and time?

Further Reading and Viewing

A fortieth anniversary special edition DVD of the film was released in 2004, including fresh documentaries and a compelling interview with former Secretary of Defense Robert McNamara. One might also compare the film *Fail Safe* (1964), which also addressed a nuclear accident and was in production at the same time as *Dr. Strangelove*—but contained nothing funny.

La bataille d'Alger (*The Battle of Algiers*)

Film Data

Year: 1966
Director: Gillo Pontecorvo
Screenplay: Franco Solinas
Music: Ennio Morricone
Length: 121 minutes
Rating: No rating

Connection to *The Cultures of the West* by Clifford R. Backman

Chapter 27: "A Theater of the Absurd, 1945–1968"

Preview

The simple musical tune of *The Battle of Algiers* has resonated throughout Western and global society for the past several decades, and the film is justifiably considered one of the most compelling and profound cinematic statements of the twentieth century. Pontecorvo's masterpiece was filmed in Algeria after the outcome of its struggle for independence from France had been determined, and it was inspired by the memoirs of an FLN (National Liberation Front) commander, who appears in the film as a lead character. However, the main setting of the film is in 1956 and 1957, chronicling a wave of assassinations of police officers in Algiers, bombings and reprisals in the European quarter and the Casbah, and the French suppression of a general strike in the city. The achievement of the film is unmatched in its combination of the techniques of a documentarian and a cinematic storyteller.

Pontecorvo came to maturity in Fascist Italy, but, due to the imposition of the virulently anti-Semitic race laws in 1938 and afterward, he was unable to secure a university education. Moving to France as a tennis champion, he met several cultural giants like Picasso, Stravinsky, and Jean-Paul Sartre and heroic veterans of the Spanish Civil War. When war broke out, Pontecorvo returned to Italy and was the leader of Communist youth in anti-Fascist resistance. Many of his films reflect the experience of fighting for freedom, as a proud and determined man of the left, and yet they also reveal the human cost of total commitment to a righteous cause. He has continued to revisit the themes of resistance and collaboration in a host of contexts and periods, even in his many unfinished or abandoned projects, but his reputation was made in *The Battle of Algiers* and his perspective on violence and terrorism, in a Middle Eastern country, is as incisive as ever.

In terms of filmmaking, Pontecorvo followed the radical strategy of casting amateurs for nearly all the main parts. He was more concerned, he noted, to employ the right faces, and not to draw on the talents of professional actors. The grainy film style was also deliberate, giving the impression of absolute realism and a documentary feel to the piece. But perhaps the most amazing elements of the film are its musical cues, composed and arranged by Pontecorvo's friend Ennio Morricone. A short tune is repeated in various registers, sometimes softly and sometimes building to a crescendo, and, in a brilliant stroke, a Bach theme plays over the scenes of devastation in a bombed Arab building and reappears over the scenes of bombed sites in the European quarter. Visually, musically, and literally, the people of the world are the same, and every death matters, regardless of the justice of its cause.

Recommended Scenes

➢ The film opens with a searing scene of an interrogation by torture, between 00:01:33 and 00:09:54. A weeping and shaking man reveals the location of Ali La Pointe's hideout to the French military, and a raid discovers four people, three adults and a child, hiding behind a wall. The scene dissolves into Ali La Pointe's memories since 1954, when he began his association with the FLN and the Algerian resistance generally. Accounting for the sources of Ali's rage, the film shows him being tripped by and then punching a French man, and a list of his "crimes" against the French occupiers is read out.

➢ The FLN has created a culture of resistance and is already regulating the lives of Algerians, presiding over marriages and harassing drunks and drug abusers in their community, 00:22:18 through 00:27:08. In a series of coordinated attacks, they assassinate police officers and seize their weapons.

➢ Bodies of women and children are picked out of the smoking ruins of a bombed-out building in the Arab quarter, to the accompanying strains of a beautiful Bach chamber piece, 00:38:00 through 00:41:40.

➤ The tension-filled and mesmerizing highlight of the film involves the bombing of three French sites, a café, a bar, and an Air France office, with the agency of three women carrying bags, 00:47:16 through 00:57:55. The most remarkable element in this brilliant sequence involves one of the terrorists glancing around the café at the people, men, women, and children, who are about to be blown up in the explosion. The French military is called in, and a biography of their commander, Philippe Mathieu, is given. Mathieu had been, ironically, a brave fighter in the Free French resistance to Nazi occupation during the War.

➤ A general strike begins, and Mathieu answers reporters' questions about his plans and tactics, 01:12:45 through 01:14:22. Interestingly, he complains about Sartre ("Why are they always born on the other side?" he asks), and one might recall Sartre's translation of *The Trojan Women* and his references to the FLN and the suffering of Algerian civilians. In the meantime, Mathieu is supervising the torture of members of the FLN network, hoping to obtain information about the higher echelons.

➤ A boy grabs a microphone and encourages the strikers, prompting an ululation of support from the women in the Casbah, 01:16:17 through 01:20:58.

➤ Scenes of torture are set to organ music, and Mathieu justifies his tactics in the name of national security and public order, 01:33:10 through 01:38:52.

➤ The scene reverts to the beginning of the film, with the four people in hiding behind a wall. The French attach explosives to the wall and prepare to blow it up. The bombs detonate, and the film ends with descriptions of the eventual independence of Algeria and a woman dancing in jubilation at that point, 01:49:02 through 02:00:40.

Discussion Questions

1. How does the film underscore the similarity of people in the European quarter of Algiers and in the Casbah?

2. How does the film specifically compare Ali La Pointe and Philippe Mathieu?

3. Does *The Battle of Algiers* justify terrorism?

Further Reading and Viewing

The three-disc Criterion Collection version of this film released in 2004 is essential viewing. It contains a series of documentaries, many of them made in the wake of 9/11 and the invasion of Iraq, drawing illuminating and controversial parallels between past and present.

Network

Film Data

Year: 1976
Director: Sidney Lumet
Created by: Paddy Chayefsky
Length: 121 minutes
Rating: R

Connection to *The Cultures of the West* by Clifford R. Backman

Chapter 28: "Something to Believe In, 1945–1988"

Preview

The presence of television in our lives is so ubiquitous and so commonplace that we cannot fully appreciate how radically this technology has transformed Western civilization. Throughout its history, television has competed with the cinema for attention, but the best investigation of television and its power to alter human thought and culture can be found in the 1976 film *Network*.

This sardonic film was the brainchild of Paddy Chayefsky, who had worked for many years in the television industry and had begun work on a screenplay about television news programs in the early 1970s. Specifically reacting to the potential takeover of the ABC network by a worldwide corporation, Chayefsky realized that a profit-driven conglomerate would probably be unwilling to carry an unprofitable division, as television news had always been. Predicting the future in an uncanny way, he understood that news would have to become an entertainment proposition, driven to ever more shocking presentations in order to secure ratings and, thereby, commercial revenue.

The film also predicts the advent of globalization, reality television shows, and our contemporary entertainment culture. As such, it is perhaps even more a document for our time than it was in the 1970s. In an appearance on the Dinah Shore show shortly after the film's release, Chayefsky denied that he had a "reformist" agenda in composing the screenplay. He commented that his central question was, "When do we say human life is more important than your lousy dollar?," and he went on to speculate that one day there would be televised gladiatorial games, something on the order of "*Colosseum 77.*"

Chayefsky was aided in realizing his vision by the director Sidney Lumet, with whom he had worked at CBS television, and by a circle of perfectly cast actors in both the major and the minor roles. Despite being British, Peter Finch indelibly impersonated an American "mad prophet of the airwaves," and Faye Dunaway was utterly convincing as the callous embodiment of television itself. Nevertheless, the strongest performances may have been by Ned Beatty, as the prophet of globalization who explains how the world works, and by Beatrice Straight, as a wife who voices all of her emotions as her husband leaves her for another woman. The film deserves to be viewed again and again, and then one should follow Howard Beale's advice and turn off the TV.

Recommended Scenes

➤ Howard Beale, anchor of the UBS network news program, is fired by his friend and superior Max Schumacher, and together they laugh about the idea of programming a "suicide of the week," an "execution of the week," or a "terrorist of the week." It still comes as a shock, however, when Beale announces that he will blow his brains out on the air next Tuesday, 00:00:13 through 00:08:01.

➤ At a programming meeting, Diana Christensen develops her idea of creating a television program around an act of real terrorism each week. She declares that the viewing public "wants someone to articulate their rage." Howard Beale continues to do this, between 00:13:25 and 00:20:08.

➤ The most famous—and endlessly referenced—scene in the film unspools Beale's "I'm as mad as hell" speech, between 00:52:21 and 01:01:02. Notice the calm reaction of the station's security guard when Beale comments, "I must make my witness."

➤ A revamped Howard Beale show includes a soothsayer and a segment hosted by "Mata Hari and her Skeletons in the Closet." Beale begins to tell the truth about television, between 01:02:20 and 01:07:05.

➤ Max falls back into his affair with Diana, and he informs his wife of the relationship in a harrowing scene. A little gem of comedy follows, as a terrorist cell bickers with the network's lawyers over distribution rights and script approval for their program, 01:11:48 through 01:21:28.

➢ When Howard Beale attempts to stop a corporate merger involving UBS, Arthur Jensen delivers a fire-and-brimstone sermon on capitalism, 01:31:53 through 01:37:45.

➢ UBS executives calmly plan the televised murder of Beale and assess its tie-in value to their other programming. The assassination unfolds, with the commentary that Beale was "the first known instance of a man being killed because of lousy ratings," 01:53:40 through 01:59:35.

Discussion Questions

1. Would a corporate executive be justified in insisting that the news division be profitable?

2. Is Howard Beale's insistence that "You've got to get mad!" productive advice?

3. In 1976, when Arthur Jensen declared, "Corporations are nations today," was he correct? Would that statement be more accurate today?

Further Reading and Viewing

For the film's thirtieth anniversary in 2006, a two-disc special edition was released, including an extensive making-of documentary and a remarkable interview with Paddy Chayefsky by Dinah Shore.

Entre les murs (The Class)

Film Data

Year: 2008
Director: Laurent Cantet
Based on the novel by François Bégaudeau
Length: 130 minutes
Rating: PG-13

Connection to *The Cultures of the West* by Clifford R. Backman

Chapter 30: "Hearts and Minds Going Forward, 2001–present"

Preview

Within the Walls (or, in the English version of the title, *The Class*) is a filmed version of François Bégaudeau's experiences as a Parisian schoolteacher. In the course of his teaching, Bégaudeau had encountered a rich—but challenging—mélange of students of various ethnic and religious backgrounds and with various levels of ability and self-discipline. Playing himself in the film as Monsieur Marin, Bégaudeau drew on his own career and, even more interestingly, interacted with adolescents who were for the most part non-actors and had been encouraged to improvise portions of their performance.

The resulting film poignantly and powerfully conveys the issues and controversies that have arisen in an ostensibly and increasingly multicultural Western Europe. Several nations have been forced to confront their abuses in the colonial period while assimilating, or while resisting the assimilation of, substantial ethnic minorities in their large cities. Simmering frustration and hostility to (at least perceived) racism exploded into a series of riots in Paris's *banlieue* (suburbs) in 2005. Young rioters set cars on fire and were forcibly subdued by the police, and then, in the summer of 2011, a similar spate of violence erupted in London and other British cities in response to the police shooting of a black teenager.

As so often, the perpetrators and the victims of this sort of violence have been young, and most frequently young men. A school is often the clearest manifestation of a society's aspirations as well as its hatreds, and *The Class* explores these issues through the eyes of an idealistic teacher, but one who is not perfect and makes several errors of judgment. Through his—and the school's—dealings with a single troublesome male student, M. Marin symbolizes some of the difficulties that impede understanding across religious and ethnic lines in today's multicultural Europe. In 2010, Chancellor Angela Merkel declared, "*'Multikulti' ist tot*," "Multicultural education and cultural policy is dead." If this is true, the scene of that death may be "between the walls" of an urban school.

Recommended Scenes

➢ A new school year opens in an inner-city Parisian "*lycée*" (middle-to-high school), but the teachers are already expressing their doubts and fears for the upcoming term, 00:04:34 through 00:07:48.

➢ A student objects to M. Marin's use of the name "Bill" in his grammatical examples, and she proposes that he use names like "Rachid" or "Ahmed" in its place, 00:12:30 through 00:15:09. As in most of the scenes that concern grammar and proper usage (this is a French class), many of the students feel that they are "not French" and that their particular cultural experiences are not represented in the dominant culture (represented here by their teacher).

➢ After another struggle over "sequence of tenses," during which students complain that "no one talks like that anymore, not even my grandmother," one of M. Marin's colleagues briefly breaks down in frustration in the teachers' lounge, 00:26:37 through 00:36:46.

➢ The central story of the film, involving a back-row student called Souleymane, whose family has emigrated from Mali, begins to emerge. M. Marin begins to make tentative steps of progress with him, and Souleymane appears to be reaching out to the concepts M. Marin is introducing, 01:02:43 through 01:12:00.

➢ Souleymane again becomes disruptive in class and is sent to the principal's office, 01:21:40 through 01:23:35.

➢ After a heated exchange in the class among several students, Souleymane flares up in anger, unable to control his hostility, and accidentally injures another student, 01:31:20 through 01:42:20.

> ➤ A disciplinary hearing is held concerning the matter of Souleymane, after which the boy is expelled from the school and will be sent to another (or, perhaps, to his family's home in Mali). The students are asked what they have learned this year, and one of the girls speaks about Plato's *Republic* and what she has learned from reading about Socrates. A soccer match seems to hint at better future for the remaining students in the class, between 01:50:50 and 02:07:02.

Discussion Questions

1. How do discussions of grammar result in discussions of racism in French society?

2. What does the discussion of the assigned reading, *The Diary of Anne Frank*, reveal?

3. What makes the experiences of Wei, the Chinese student who is in danger of being deported, different from those of Souleymane?

Further Reading and Viewing

Perhaps the best avenue would be to reflect on one's own experience in high school, and what messages were conveyed by the teachers and the design of the institution as a whole.